# ASIA-PACIFIC TRADE FACILITATION REPORT 2021

## SUPPLY CHAINS OF CRITICAL GOODS AMID THE COVID-19 PANDEMIC

### DISRUPTIONS, RECOVERY, AND RESILIENCE

OCTOBER 2021

ESCAP 75
MOVING FORWARD TOGETHER

ADB

# CONTENTS

# TABLES, FIGURES, AND BOXES

## DIGITAL AND SUSTAINABLE TRADE FACILITATION

### TABLES

### FIGURES

### BOX

## SUPPLY CHAINS OF CRITICAL GOODS AMID THE COVID-19 PANDEMIC—DISRUPTIONS, RECOVERY, AND RESILIENCE

### TABLES

### FIGURES

## BOXES

# FOREWORD

By Armida Salsiah Alisjahbana, ESCAP

The COVID-19 pandemic dramatically reduced international trade last year and significantly disrupted global value chains, complicating progress in Asia and the Pacific toward sustainable development. While trade in goods has since recovered strongly, supply chains need to be made more resilient, particularly to ensure the supply of critical goods.

The *Asia-Pacific Trade Facilitation Report 2021* shows that despite COVID-19, economies in the region have managed to cut red tape to keep trade flowing, as evidenced by the results of the 2021 Global Survey on Digital and Sustainable Trade Facilitation.

Also evident is that digitalization of trade procedures has accelerated, although much more remains to be done. Cross-border trade digitalization has great potential to help countries in Asia and the Pacific access critical goods, especially those most vulnerable to trade uncertainty and crisis.

The report indicates that further acceleration of digital trade facilitation implementation could cut average trade costs in the region by more than 13 per cent. It suggests that the Framework Agreement on Facilitation of Cross-Border Paperless Trade in Asia and the Pacific—a United Nations treaty that entered into force in early 2021—provides a dedicated, inclusive, and capacity-building-focused intergovernmental platform to pursue this agenda.

The report also highlights the need for more holistic and inclusive trade facilitation strategies in the region to ensure that groups and sectors with special needs benefit from the trade recovery. Measures are specifically needed to support small and medium-sized enterprises, women, and the agricultural sector to make the recovery more sustainable.

I am confident that this new study will support countries in designing evidence-based measures and policies to make international trade more efficient and inclusive and to foster greater regional cooperation for Asia and the Pacific. With this our region can recover stronger and better from the pandemic.

**Armida Salsiah Alisjahbana**
Under-Secretary-General of the United Nations and Executive Secretary
United Nations Economic and Social Commission for Asia and the Pacific

# FOREWORD

By Bambang Susantono, ADB

The coronavirus disease (COVID-19) pandemic has had severe impacts on multiple sectors of economies in Asia and the Pacific, as declining international trade flows and lower demand slashed operations in ports, transport hubs, and logistics facilities. While economic recovery is under way in 2021, it remains precarious and uncertain as new variants of the virus emerge.

As such, the COVID-19 pandemic has exposed the vulnerabilities of global and regional value chains as it has disrupted supply, particularly for essential goods such as personal protective equipment (PPE), vaccines, and food. Export restrictions, strict border controls for customs clearance, and drastic public health measures, among other factors, explain the dramatic impact.

The disruptions of the outbreak have also underscored the important role trade facilitation plays in economies and will play in the recovery. The pandemic also revealed the need for digital, paperless trade procedures to facilitate cross-border movement of critical goods during global health emergencies, while maintaining open trade regimes to maintain equitable access to essential goods.

This year's Asia-Pacific Trade Facilitation Report highlights the progress of trade facilitation reforms during the COVID-19 pandemic. Its special chapter on supply chains—with case studies on food supplies, PPE, and vaccines—discusses pandemic mitigation efforts. As workers fell ill amid the mobility and safety restrictions, food supplies were disrupted, especially as export bans emerged in major food crop producing countries. Likewise, for PPE, the early stages of the pandemic curtailed supplies, particularly with supply chains concentrated in a few countries and lean inventory systems as the norm. Quickly boosting production globally proved difficult. And for vaccines, with only a few countries able to manufacture them, upscaling production for global provision of this one great defense against the virus has been challenging.

This report offers policy suggestions on how to enhance supply chain resilience. The pandemic has presented an opportunity to accelerate implementation of the World Trade Organization's Trade Facilitation Agreement to reduce trade costs across the region, for example. And developing economies can benefit by implementing digital trade facilitation.

Multilateral agencies can help coordinate these efforts, provide financing and technical assistance to build institutional capacity, and help economies acquire digital infrastructure. Governments and the private sector, too, should cooperate to build business continuity plans and enhance supply chain resilience. Assistance, such as access to supply chain and trade finance, should be extended to small producers.

I hope this report will improve understanding of the impacts of the pandemic and highlight the importance of trade facilitation reforms to post-COVID-19 economic recovery and sustainable development. Greater regional cooperation is needed to harmonize all the technical and legal requirements to achieve more efficient trade procedures. We should act with urgency.

**Bambang Susantono**
Vice-President for Knowledge Management and Sustainable Development
Asian Development Bank

# ACKNOWLEDGMENTS

This publication was jointly prepared by the Regional Cooperation and Integration Division (ERCI) of the Economic Research and Regional Cooperation Department (ERCD) of the Asian Development Bank (ADB), and the Trade, Investment and Innovation Division (TIID) of the United Nations Economic and Social Commission for Asia and the Pacific (ESCAP).

Cyn-Young Park, director of ERCI, ADB and Yann Duval, chief of the Trade Policy and Facilitation Section, TIID, ESCAP led the preparation of this publication.

ESCAP provided the chapter on Digital and Trade Facilitation. The contributing authors, Chorthip Utoktham, Jiangyuan Fu, and Soo Hyun Kim, provided the analysis of new data for countries in Asia and the Pacific, collected as part of the United Nations Global Survey on Digital and Sustainable Trade Facilitation 2021. The authors are grateful to Salehin Khan and Charles Frei from the Economic Commission for Europe for supporting data collection in Central Asian countries. Ruixin Xie, Yifan Tan, and Linyi Chen provided research assistance.

ADB provided the theme chapter on Supply Chains of Critical Goods amid the COVID-19 Pandemic. Contributing authors include Kijin Kim, Benjamin Endriga, and Sanchita Basu Das. Research support was provided by Jerome Abesamis.

Kijin Kim coordinated overall production assisted by Aleli Rosario. Eric Van Zant edited the manuscript. Jan Carlo Dela Cruz created the cover design. Jonathan Yamongan did the layout and typesetting. The material was proofread by Tuesday Soriano with assistance from Carol Ongchangco and Aleli Rosario. Support for printing and publishing this report was provided by the Printing Services Unit of ADB's Office of Administrative Services and by the publishing team of the Department of Communications.

# ABBREVIATIONS

| | |
|---|---|
| ADB | Asian Development Bank |
| APEC | Asia-Pacific Economic Cooperation |
| ASEAN | Association of Southeast Asian Nations |
| COVID-19 | coronavirus disease |
| ESCAP | Economic and Social Commission for Asia and the Pacific |
| EU | European Union |
| Lao PDR | Lao People's Democratic Republic |
| PPE | personal protective equipment |
| PRC | People's Republic of China |
| SMEs | small and medium-sized enterprises |
| TFA | Trade Facilitation Agreement |
| UN | United Nations |
| WHO | World Health Organization |
| WTO | World Trade Organization |

# HIGHLIGHTS

## ■ | Digital and Sustainable Trade Facilitation in Asia and the Pacific

**Trade costs are on the rise, especially with the recent surge in shipping costs, but continuous trade facilitation implementation could help bend the trend.** International shipping costs recently surged to an all-time peak, which may further disrupt the international supply chain with its heavy reliance on sea freight transport. This recent increase has put additional pressure on already high trade costs in Asia and the Pacific. According to the United Nations Economic and Social Commission for Asia and the Pacific (ESCAP)-World Bank Trade Cost Database, trade costs in Asia and the Pacific are the highest in South Asia. Central Asia and the Pacific have made progress in reducing trade costs over the past several years but they remain high. East Asia has the lowest trade costs among all Asia and Pacific subregions, followed by the Association of Southeast Asian Nations (ASEAN) subregion.

**The 2021 Global Survey on Digital and Sustainable Trade Facilitation shows continued progress on streamlining trade procedures in Asia and the Pacific.** Despite the coronavirus disease (COVID-19) pandemic and the subsequent supply chain disruptions and the surge in shipping costs, the survey showed that the implementation of 31 general and digital trade facilitation measures rose in average across the region to 64.9% in 2021, about 6 percentage points higher than in 2019. Australia and New Zealand (96.8%) lead implementation in the region, followed by East Asia (82.5%), Southeast Asia and Timor-Leste (74.3%), the Russian Federation and Central Asia (71.4%), and South Asia, Iran, and Turkey (63.1%). The Pacific is considerably behind other subregions, with an implementation rate of 40.1%. South Asia, Iran, and Turkey made most progress, with an increase of more than 10 percentage points since 2019. The Pacific also made substantial progress, despite the significant challenges and trade disruptions due to the COVID-19 pandemic.

**Building on continuous efforts to implement Trade Facilitation Agreement (TFA)-related measures, economies in Asia and the Pacific would benefit greatly by gradually moving toward trade digitalization.** The 2021 survey shows that the World Trade Organization (WTO) TFA-related measures have been well implemented throughout the region by improving *transparency* (81.7%), streamlining the *formalities* (75.5%), and enhancing *institutional arrangement and cooperation* mechanisms (68.4%). On the other hand, despite continued improvement of digital infrastructure to facilitate trusted and secure sharing of trade-related data and documents in electronic form, implementation of cross-border paperless trade remains challenging with a regional average implementation rate below 40%. Implementation of bilateral and subregional paperless trade systems remain mostly at the pilot stage, although the pandemic contributed to the acceleration of digital transformation. Simulation results show that full digital trade facilitation implementation beyond the WTO TFA could cut average trade costs in the region by more than 13%. The Framework Agreement on Facilitation of Cross-Border Paperless Trade in Asia and the Pacific, a United Nations treaty which entered into force in early 2021, provides a dedicated, inclusive, and capacity-building–focused intergovernmental platform to pursue this agenda.

**More holistic and inclusive trade facilitation strategies are required to enhance strategies targeting groups and sectors with special needs.** Implementation of sustainable trade facilitation measures, especially those aiming for small and medium-sized enterprises (SMEs) and women, face big challenges, with average implementation rates of 41.7% and 33.3%, respectively. Implementation of agricultural trade facilitation has higher implementation rate at 58.5%. Measures specifically supporting SMEs and women should be adopted and developed further, building inclusive and resilient trade facilitation mechanisms, to support the achievement of the Sustainable Development Goals. The report also shows a high positive correlation between digital and sustainable dimensions of trade facilitation, indicating that synergies could be achieved by enhancing both dimensions.

**Trade facilitation has emerged as an effective tool to mitigate the devastating effect of COVID-19 on trade by simplifying and digitalizing formalities in international trade.** The pandemic highlighted the role of trade facilitation in ensuring swift movement of medical and other essential goods. The Trade Facilitation in Times of Crisis section of the survey shows that most governments in the region have swiftly implemented a number of short-term crisis measures in response to the pandemic and subsequent trade disruptions. The implementation rate of crisis-related trade facilitation measures only stands at 55.7%, on average, essentially because many countries still lack long-term trade facilitation plans to enhance preparedness for future crises.

## Overall Implementation of Trade Facilitation Measures in 46 Asia and Pacific Countries

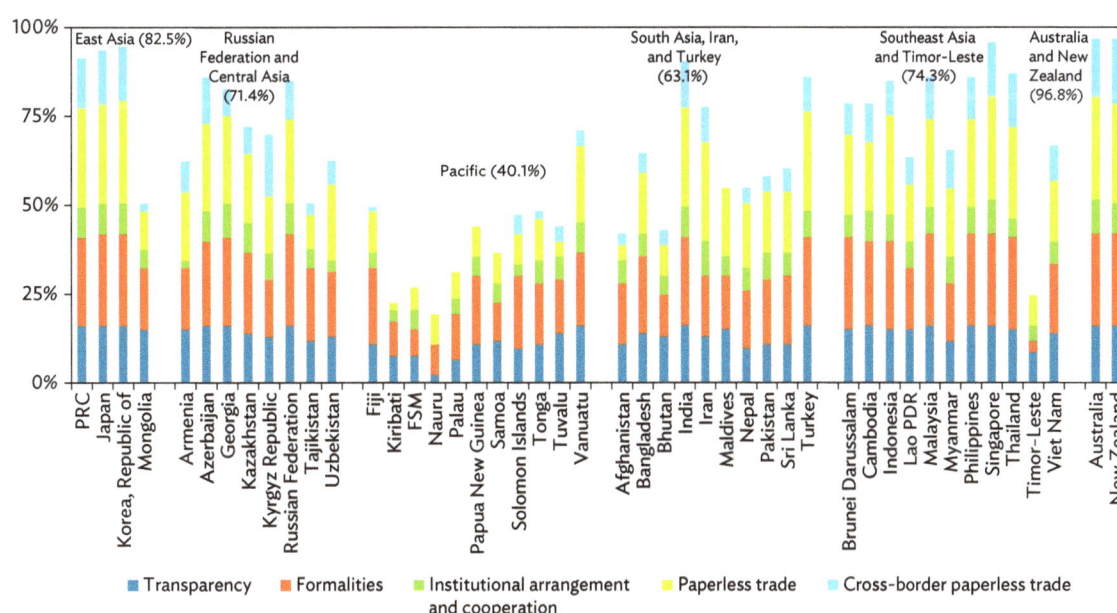

East Asia (82.5%); Russian Federation and Central Asia (71.4%); Pacific (40.1%); South Asia, Iran, and Turkey (63.1%); Southeast Asia and Timor-Leste (74.3%); Australia and New Zealand (96.8%)

Legend: ■ Transparency  ■ Formalities  ■ Institutional arrangement and cooperation  ■ Paperless trade  ■ Cross-border paperless trade

FSM = Federated States of Micronesia, Lao PDR = Lao People's Democratic Republic, PRC = People's Republic of China.

Note: Among the 58 measures surveyed across the United Nations regional commissions, three measures including *electronic submission of sea cargo manifests, alignment of working days and hours with neighboring countries at border crossings,* and *alignment of formalities and procedures with neighboring countries at border crossings* are excluded when calculating the overall score as they are not relevant to all countries surveyed. Four *transit facilitation* measures are also excluded for the same reason. Additionally, *sustainable trade facilitation* and *other trade facilitation* are excluded as these newly added groups of measures were not included in the earlier surveys, for comparison.

Source: UN Global Survey on Digital and Sustainable Trade Facilitation. untfsurvey.org.

# ■ | Theme Chapter: Supply Chains of Critical Goods amid the COVID-19 Pandemic

## Supply Chain Capabilities and Vulnerability

**The COVID-19 pandemic laid bare the vulnerabilities of globalization and global supply chains, as concentrated trade networks and limiting inventories helped weaken them.** High global value chain participation left Asia and the Pacific vulnerable to restrictive trade measures. A shortage of financing worsened resource constraints. And even though trade policy is a crucial anchor for the smooth functioning of international production networks, many economies imposed trade-restricting policies on medical and agriculture goods.

**Addressing these vulnerabilities required strengthening the capabilities of supply chains in various areas.** Building on past lessons, existing national and regional mechanisms and initiatives helped raise capacity for strengthening collaboration and making supply chains more efficient. Nonetheless, new measures were urgently needed even as existing ones adjusted to the unprecedented crisis.

## Vaccines and Personal Protective Equipment

**Limited vaccine supply, logistics challenges, lack of funding and staff resources for vaccination, and vaccine hesitancy have hampered efforts to quickly immunize a meaningful share of populations.** The geographic concentration of major manufacturers of vaccines and personal protective equipment (PPE) leaves supply exposed to localized shocks and changes in national security laws and trade policies. At the onset of the pandemic, the world encountered critical shortages of PPE and other essential medical devices, aggravated by export bans on medical supplies and PPE in some cases to curb local shortages. Securing sufficient supplies of vaccines and PPE remains an important challenge in many parts of the world in vaccine rollouts and in sustaining essential health services.

**Developing economies need to address several logistics issues to successfully immunize their populations.** Low air transport capacity should be addressed as closed airports and lack of flights during the pandemic have created bottlenecks. Shipments must remain secure from tampering and theft at all points in the supply chain of medical goods. Well-coordinated and timely regulatory approvals, inspection, and clearance by customs and health authorities are essential. And adequate, temperature-controlled supply chains need to be secured. Yet, temperature-controlled supply chains are limited in developing economies, making it hard to accommodate the various temperature requirements of the different vaccines.

## Food Supply Chains

**During COVID-19, food supply chains came under pressure amid domestic and international disruptions.** Domestically, travel restrictions prevented local and migrant workers from moving to farms, processing, and packaging facilities, many of which were closed due to quarantine requirements and sick workers. Access to farm inputs became challenging. Restrictions in urban transportation and logistics services impaired movement of goods, causing large-scale wastage, particularly for high-value perishable farm products. Demand shocks were also felt as many farmers were left with no buyers as restaurants, hotels, and schools closed.

**Cross-border transport restrictions disrupted the global supply chain.** Maritime transport was particularly hampered by disruption in port facilities, which became congested amid a lack of workers and transport to clear cargo. Compulsory health screening of crews and additional customs documentation added to time and cost. All these left refrigerated storage unavailable for fresh foods, causing perishables to spoil and increasing food waste. Export bans on basic food items further strained regional supply chains.

## Policy Implications

**Global and regional cooperation.** The COVID-19 pandemic highlighted the importance of prompt international support and cooperation for continuous supplies of critical medical goods, even more so given the need for doing so sustainably and inclusively. Many regional cooperation measures came into practice to mitigate the adversities. About two-thirds of 20 Asia-Pacific Economic Cooperation (APEC) economies implemented new trade facilitation measures to mitigate supply chain disruptions. And almost all APEC economies expedited implementation of measures to simplify customs procedures, similar to priority lanes for essential goods. To assure equitable vaccine distribution, the COVAX facility was instituted as a credible global health cooperation, while the Asia Pacific Vaccine Access Facility of the Asian Development Bank (ADB) was designed to support equitable distribution of COVID-19 vaccines among its developing member countries.

**Open trade and trade facilitation.** Trade openness remains a key element for economic recovery. Countries should refrain from using export restrictions and other nontariff measures. They should also increase transparency on trade restrictions implemented during and in the aftermath of COVID-19. Trade facilitation measures helped ease the trade flow of essential goods during the peak of the pandemic. As the health crisis continues, ramping up trade facilitation becomes crucial. Countries should prioritize implementation of the WTO TFA and the related UN treaty on cross-border paperless trade in Asia and the Pacific to accelerate recovery post-COVID-19.

**Digital technology.** Globally and regionally, digital technologies need to be used more to enhance monitoring and strengthening of supply chains. For instance, digital technologies can help in monitoring PPE use and distribution and centralizing visibility of orders. Digital systems can monitor vaccine procurement and distribution and keep track of vaccinated populations globally. As the pandemic has quickened the move to digital, paperless trading, work is needed to leverage information and communication technologies to streamline customs procedures and electronic exchange of information, implement national and regional single windows for document submission and clearance, and introduce e-registration of travel documents.

**Assistance targeted to vulnerable economies and groups.** International efforts should include targeted assistance to vulnerable economies and sectors. Reforms in agriculture can include targeted support to smallholder farmers, including improving their access to digital infrastructure and training, rural financing, marketing opportunities, and value chain infrastructure. As many PPE supply manufacturers are micro, small and medium-sized enterprises and severely impacted by supply chain disruptions, trade finance programs help these small producers trade using the supply chain. Stronger regional cooperation, meanwhile, can also help low-income economies gain access to vaccines.

**Role of multilateral institutions.** Multilateral institutions have played key roles in responding to the pandemic and cushioning its health and economic impacts. To facilitate seamless and equitable distribution, the World Customs Organization and the World Health Organization (WHO) jointly developed a harmonized list of vaccines and related products such as syringes, swabs, and freezing equipment to guide customs and border agencies in facilitating imports of these products. These institutions also responded earlier in creating a harmonized list for PPE and disinfectants. In response to the shortage of trade finance, the WTO and major multilateral banks including the International Finance Corporation, European Bank for Reconstruction and Development, ADB, and others in July 2020 declared a crisis in trade finance and allocated resources to mitigate. Multilateral institutions also play a key role in advancing free trade and helping countries implement trade facilitation measures. Multilateral development banks should continue to play a coordinating role to support regional trade facilitation policies. ADB's subregional programs provide an institutional venue for these initiatives. Helping economies build regulatory capacity and acquire digital infrastructure should also be supported.

# DIGITAL AND SUSTAINABLE TRADE FACILITATION IN ASIA AND THE PACIFIC*

\* This section is based on the Digital and Sustainable Trade Facilitation in the Asia-Pacific Regional Report 2021 done by ESCAP. See https://www.unescap.org/kp/2021/untf-survey-2021-regional.

# 1 Trade Costs and Trade Facilitation in Asia and the Pacific: State of Play

## 1.1 | Trade Costs: Subregional Trends

The latest data published in the United Nations Economic and Social Commission for Asia and the Pacific (ESCAP)–World Bank Trade Cost Database show the overall average cost of trading goods among the three largest European economies (EU-3) as approximately 41% tariff equivalent (Table 1). The closest comparison of the Asia and Pacific performance to the EU-3 benchmark is intraregional trade costs among the People's Republic of China (PRC), Japan, and the Republic of Korea (East Asia-3) (57% tariff equivalent), followed by Association of Southeast Asian Nations (ASEAN) members (77% tariff equivalent). The highest intraregional trade cost is observed among four large members of the South Asian Association for Regional Cooperation (SAARC-4) (roughly 128% tariff equivalent).

**Table 1:** Intra- and Extra-Regional Comprehensive Trade Costs, 2014–2019 (excluding tariff costs)

| Region | ASEAN-4 (%) | East Asia-3 (%) | Russian Fed. and Central Asia-3 (%) | Pacific-2 (%) | SAARC-4 (%) | AUS-NZL (%) | EU-3 (%) |
|---|---|---|---|---|---|---|---|
| **ASEAN-4** | 76.7 (3.9) | 79.4 (6.8) | 319.0 (−1.7) | 308.5 (−3.8) | 135.2 (5.1) | 103.3 (5.0) | 103.8 (−3.2) |
| **East Asia-3** | 79.4 (6.8) | 56.9 (9.8) | 168.2 (−3.6) | 241.6 (−14.0) | 125.4 (1.0) | 89.0 (2.1) | 85.2 (0.3) |
| **Russian Federation and Central Asia-3** | 319.0 (−1.7) | 168.2 (−3.6) | 110.6 (−8.6) | 417.1 (13.7) | 268.7 (−8.5) | 318.8 (−8.5) | 148.2 (−2.7) |
| **Pacific-3** | 308.5 (−3.8) | 241.6 (−14.0) | 417.1 (13.7) | 117.9 (−12.6) | 409.8 (3.2) | 117.3 (1.3) | 397.9 (−3.0) |
| **SAARC-4** | 135.2 (5.1) | 125.4 (1.0) | 268.7 (−8.5) | 409.8 (3.2) | 128.4 (13.4) | 138.0 (0.2) | 113.7 (−0.5) |
| **AUS-NZL** | 103.3 (5.0) | 89.0 (2.1) | 318.8 (−8.5) | 117.3 (1.3) | 138.0 (0.2) | 54.0 (3.6) | 105.8 (−1.1) |
| **EU-3** | 103.8 (−3.2) | 85.2 (0.3) | 148.2 (−2.7) | 397.9 (−3.0) | 113.7 (−0.5) | 105.8 (−1.1) | 41.4 (−5.9) |
| **United States** | 86.6 (2.0) | 66.2 (5.4) | 190.5 (7.1) | 199.8 (−4.5) | 114.2 (3.6) | 99.7 (0.5) | 66.7 (0.1) |

ASEAN = Association of Southeast Asian Nations, AUS = Australia, EU = European Union, NZL = New Zealand, SAARC = South Asian Association for Regional Cooperation.

Notes: Trade costs may be interpreted as tariff equivalents. Percentage changes in trade costs between 2008–2013 and 2014–2019 are in parentheses.

ASEAN-4: Indonesia, Malaysia, the Philippines, Thailand; East Asia-3: the People's Republic of China, Japan, the Republic of Korea; EU-3: Germany, France, the United Kingdom; SAARC-4: Bangladesh, India, Pakistan, Sri Lanka; Pacific-3: Fiji, Tonga, Samoa; Central Asia-3: Georgia, Kazakhstan, the Kyrgyz Republic.

Source: ESCAP-World Bank Trade Cost Database, updated July 2021. https://www.unescap.org/resources/escap-world-bank-trade-cost-database (accessed September 2021).

High trade costs, as a result of the coronavirus disease (COVID-19) pandemic, still persist and the effect is not limited only to the Asia and Pacific region. Global international shipping costs have recently surged to an all-time peak, which may disrupt international supply chains in the long term, as 80% of traded goods depends on sea freight transport. Despite the surge in international shipping costs, recent developments in streamlining trade facilitation are intact, which could partially suppress such increase in cost of trading across borders.[1]

## 1.2 | Implementation of Digital and Sustainable Trade Facilitation Measures

### 1.2.1  Status of Implementation

The regional state of implementation of trade facilitation presented in the chapter is based on the results of the fourth United Nations Global Survey on Digital and Sustainable Trade Facilitation, conducted in 2021.[2] The Global Survey started in 2015 with all United Nations regional commissions, then other international organizations joined in 2017. The Global Survey built on earlier efforts from Asia and the Pacific, with the regional survey on the implementation of trade facilitation and paperless trade conducted in 2012 by the ESCAP secretariat during the 4th Asia–Pacific Trade Facilitation Forum, co-organized by ESCAP and the Asian Development Bank (ADB). With the reliable, detailed, and regularly updated data on the implementation of both traditional and more forward-looking trade facilitation measures, the Global Survey supports development of evidence-based trade facilitation policies for resilient and inclusive trade.[3]

The 2021 survey includes 58 trade facilitation measures under 4 groups and 11 subgroups (Table 2). The first group—general trade facilitation measures—comprises a number of World Trade Organization (WTO) Trade Facilitation Agreement (TFA) measures, grouped into the subgroups *transparency, formalities, institutional arrangement and cooperation,* and *transit facilitation.* Two subgroups fall under the group of *digital trade facilitation measures* which are related to the UN treaty on cross-border paperless trade (Box 1): *paperless trade* and *cross-border paperless trade.* Subgroups on *trade facilitation for SMEs, agricultural trade facilitation,* and *women in trade facilitation* are under the group of *sustainable trade facilitation measures.* To keep abreast of the latest trade facilitation developments in trade finance and against the background of the COVID-19 pandemic, *other trade facilitation* group includes two subgroups: *trade finance facilitation*[4] and *trade facilitation in times of crisis.*

---

[1]    See articles from UNCTAD (2021a) or (2021b) for more details.

[2]    Regional groupings used here are defined as follows: East Asia includes the PRC, Japan, the Republic of Korea, and Mongolia; Central Asia includes Armenia, Azerbaijan, Georgia, Kazakhstan, the Kyrgyz Republic, Tajikistan, and Uzbekistan; the Pacific includes Fiji, Kiribati, the Federated States of Micronesia, Nauru, Palau, Papua New Guinea, Samoa, Solomon Islands, Tonga, Tuvalu, and Vanuatu; South Asia includes Afghanistan, Bangladesh, Bhutan, India, Maldives, Nepal, Pakistan, and Sri Lanka; Southeast Asia includes Brunei Darussalam, Cambodia, Indonesia, the Lao People's Democratic Republic (Lao PDR), Malaysia, Myanmar, the Philippines, Singapore, Thailand, and Viet Nam; landlocked developing countries include Afghanistan, Armenia, Azerbaijan, Bhutan, Kazakhstan, the Kyrgyz Republic, the Lao PDR, Mongolia, Nepal, Tajikistan, and Uzbekistan; least developed countries include Afghanistan, Bangladesh, Bhutan, Cambodia, Kiribati, the Lao PDR, Myanmar, Nepal, Solomon Islands, Timor-Leste, Tuvalu, and Vanuatu; small island developing states include Fiji, Kiribati, Maldives, the Federated States of Micronesia, Nauru, Palau, Papua New Guinea, Samoa, Solomon Islands, Timor-Leste, Tonga, Tuvalu, and Vanuatu.

[3]    The survey results are available at https://untfsurvey.org.

[4]    Trade finance facilitation, developed in cooperation with the International Chamber of Commerce, was an optional subgroup in the 2019 survey and three regional commissions, i.e., ESCAP, Economic and Social Commission for Western Asia, and Economic Commission for Europe used this optional subgroup. In 2021, this subgroup is updated and surveyed across all regions.

**Table 2:  Grouping of Trade Facilitation Measures and Correspondence with Trade Facilitation Agreement Articles**

| Groups | Subgroups | Measures | Relevant TFA Articles |
|---|---|---|---|
| General Trade Facilitation | Transparency (5 measures) | Publication of existing import–export regulations on the internet | 1.2 |
| | | Stakeholders' consultation on new draft regulations (prior to their finalization) | 2.2 |
| | | Advance publication/notification of new trade-related regulations before their implementation (e.g., 30 days prior) | 2.1 |
| | | Advance ruling on tariff classification and origin of imported goods | 3 |
| | | Independent appeal mechanism (for traders to appeal customs rulings and the rulings of other relevant trade control agencies) | 4 |
| | Formalities (8 measures) | Risk management (for deciding whether a shipment will be physically inspected) | 7.4 |
| | | Pre-arrival processing | 7.1 |
| | | Post-clearance audits | 7.5 |
| | | Separation of release from final determination of customs duties, taxes, fees, and charges | 7.3 |
| | | Establishment and publication of average release times | 7.6 |
| | | Trade facilitation measures for authorized operators | 7.7 |
| | | Expedited shipments | 7.8 |
| | | Acceptance of copies of original supporting documents required for import, export, or transit formalities | 10.2.1 |
| | Institutional arrangement and cooperation (5 measures) | Establishment of a national trade facilitation committee or similar body | 23 |
| | | National legislative framework and/or institutional arrangements for border agencies cooperation | 8 |
| | | Government agencies delegating border controls to customs authorities | |
| | | Alignment of working days and hours with neighboring countries at border crossings | 8.2(a) |
| | | Alignment of formalities and procedures with neighboring countries at border crossings | 8.2(b) |
| | Transit facilitation (4 measures) | Transit facilitation agreement(s) with neighboring country(ies) | |
| | | Customs authorities limit the physical inspections of transit goods and use risk assessment | 10.5 |
| | | Supporting pre-arrival processing for transit facilitation | 11.9 |
| | | Cooperation between agencies of countries involved in transit | 11.16 |
| Digital Trade Facilitation | Paperless trade (10 measures) | Automated Customs System (e.g., ASYCUDA) | |
| | | Internet connection available to customs and other trade control agencies at border crossings | |
| | | Electronic single window system | 10.4 |
| | | Electronic submission of customs declarations | |
| | | Electronic application and issuance of import and export permits | |
| | | Electronic submission of sea cargo manifests | |
| | | Electronic submission of air cargo manifests | |
| | | Electronic application and issuance of Preferential Certificate of Origin | |
| | | E-payment of customs duties and fees | 7.2 |
| | | Electronic Application for Customs Refunds | |

*continued next page*

**Table 2:** *Continued*

| Groups | Subgroups | Measures | Relevant TFA Articles |
|---|---|---|---|
| Digital Trade Facilitation | Cross-border paperless trade (6 measures) | Laws and regulations for electronic transactions are in place (e.g., e-commerce law, e-transaction law) | |
| | | Recognized certification authority issuing digital certificates to traders to conduct electronic transactions | |
| | | Electronic exchange of customs declaration | |
| | | Electronic exchange of Certificate of Origin | |
| | | Electronic exchange of Sanitary and Phyto-Sanitary (SPS) Certificate | |
| | | Paperless collection of payment from a documentary letter of credit | |
| Sustainable Trade Facilitation | Trade facilitation for SMEs (5 measures) | Trade-related information measures for small and medium-sized enterprises (SMEs) | |
| | | SMEs in Authorized Economic Operators (AEO) scheme (i.e., government has developed specific measures that enable SMEs to more easily benefit from the AEO scheme) | |
| | | SMEs access single window (i.e., government has taken actions to make single windows more easily accessible to SMEs, e.g., by providing technical consultation and training services to SMEs on registering and using the facility.) | |
| | | SMEs in a national trade facilitation committee (i.e., government has taken actions to ensure that SMEs are well-represented and made key members of national trade facilitation committees) | |
| | | Other special measures for SMEs | |
| | Agricultural trade facilitation (4 measures) | Testing and laboratory facilities available to meet SPS standards of main trading partners | |
| | | National standards and accreditation bodies are established to facilitate compliance with SPS standards | |
| | | Electronic application and issuance of SPS certificates | |
| | | Special treatment for perishable goods at border crossings | 7.9 |
| | Women in trade facilitation (3 measures) | Trade facilitation policy/strategy to increase women's participation in trade | |
| | | Trade facilitation measures to benefit women involved in trade | |
| | | Women membership in the national trade facilitation committee or similar bodies | |
| Other Trade Facilitation | Trade finance facilitation (3 measures) | Single window facilitates traders' access to finance | |
| | | Authorities engaged in blockchain-based supply chain project covering trade finance | |
| | | Variety of trade finance services available | |
| | Trade facilitation in times of crisis (5 measures) | Agency in place to manage trade facilitation in times of crises and emergencies | |
| | | Online publication of emergency trade facilitation measures | |
| | | Coordination between countries on emergency trade facilitation measures | |
| | | Additional trade facilitation measures to facilitate trade in times of emergencies | |
| | | Plan in place to facilitate trade during future crises | |

TFA = Trade Facilitation Agreement.

Source: UN Global Survey on Digital and Sustainable Trade Facilitation. untfsurvey.org.

> **Box:** **Framework Agreement on Facilitation of Cross-Border Paperless Trade in Asia and the Pacific: An Update**
>
> The Framework Agreement on Facilitation of Cross-Border Paperless Trade in Asia and the Pacific, a United Nations treaty, aims to promote cross-border paperless trade by enabling the exchange and mutual recognition of trade-related data and documents in electronic form and facilitating interoperability among national and subregional single windows and/or other paperless trade systems. It is designed as an inclusive and enabling platform that will benefit all participating economies regardless of where they stand in trade facilitation or single window/paperless trade implementation.
>
> Economic and Social Commission for Asia and the Pacific (ESCAP) members adopted the treaty in 2016 and it entered into force on 20 February 2021, doing so 90 days after the date on which the governments of at least five ESCAP member states deposited their instruments of ratification or accession, as per Article 19 of the agreement. Azerbaijan acceded in March 2018 and the Philippines in December 2019. The Islamic Republic of Iran ratified in May 2020, Bangladesh in October 2020, and the People's Republic of China, as the 5th country, in November 2020. Armenia and Cambodia signed in 2017. Several other ESCAP member states are completing their domestic processes for accession.
>
> Several benefits derive from the agreement. First, it enables countries to send a clear signal of high-level commitment and vision of the country's leadership in harnessing the benefits from trade digitalization and to engage in the fast-growing digital economy. Second, it provides parties increased opportunities for capacity building through training, workshops and knowledge-sharing platforms, as well as easier access to information, knowledge and resources to achieve full digital implementation of the World Trade Organization Trade Facilitation Agreement. Ultimately, it is expected to bring substantial efficiency gains by enabling electronic exchange of data and documents, which could cut trade costs by up to 25% and enhance regulatory compliance.
>
> Source: ESCAP. 2021a. Framework Agreement on Facilitation of Cross-border Paperless Trade in Asia and the Pacific. https://www.unescap.org/kp/cpta.

The survey includes measures specified in the WTO TFA as well as complementary and forward-looking measures on digital, sustainable, and other areas that go beyond the conventional measures. Paperless trade measures, notably cross-border paperless trade, are not explicitly included in the WTO TFA, however, they would make TFA implementation more effective. Under the *sustainable trade facilitation* group, besides measures under the *agricultural trade facilitation* subgroup, most measures are not particularly specified in the WTO TFA. The *other trade facilitation* group illustrates the role of trade finance in maintaining trade flows, as well as trade facilitation measures during crisis. The latter are crucial to establish sustainable and resilient recovery to *build back better*, after the disrupted global trade and global supply chain triggered by the COVID-19 pandemic.

Between January and July of 2021, data for the fourth UN Global Survey on Digital and Sustainable Trade Facilitation was collected. For each measure, implementation level is recorded as 3 for "fully implemented," 2 for "partially implemented," 1 for "on a pilot basis," or 0 for "not implemented." Each implementation of a measure is calculated against its full score (3). Then, the average score for the set of measures is expressed by percentage. For each subgroup, a set of relevant measures is calculated.

Implementation rates of 31 general and digital trade facilitation measures included in the survey were calculated for 46 countries in Asia and the Pacific (Figure 1). The regional average implementation rate is at 64.9% according to the 2021 survey. Implementation rates vary greatly by country as well as subregion. Countries such as Australia, the PRC, India, Japan, New Zealand, the Republic of Korea, and Singapore have implementation rates of above 90%, whereas numerous Pacific countries have implementation rates of less than 30%.

Figure 2 shows trade facilitation implementation rates by subregion and groups of countries with special needs, including landlocked developing countries, least developed countries, and small island developing states. Besides Australia and New Zealand, East Asia ranks the highest average level of implementation (82.5%), followed by Southeast Asia (74.3%), the Russian Federation and Central Asia (71.4%), and South Asia, Iran, and Turkey (63.1%); the Pacific is considerably behind other subregions, with an implementation rate of 40.1% only.

**Figure 1:** **Overall Implementation of Trade Facilitation Measures in 46 Asia and Pacific Countries**

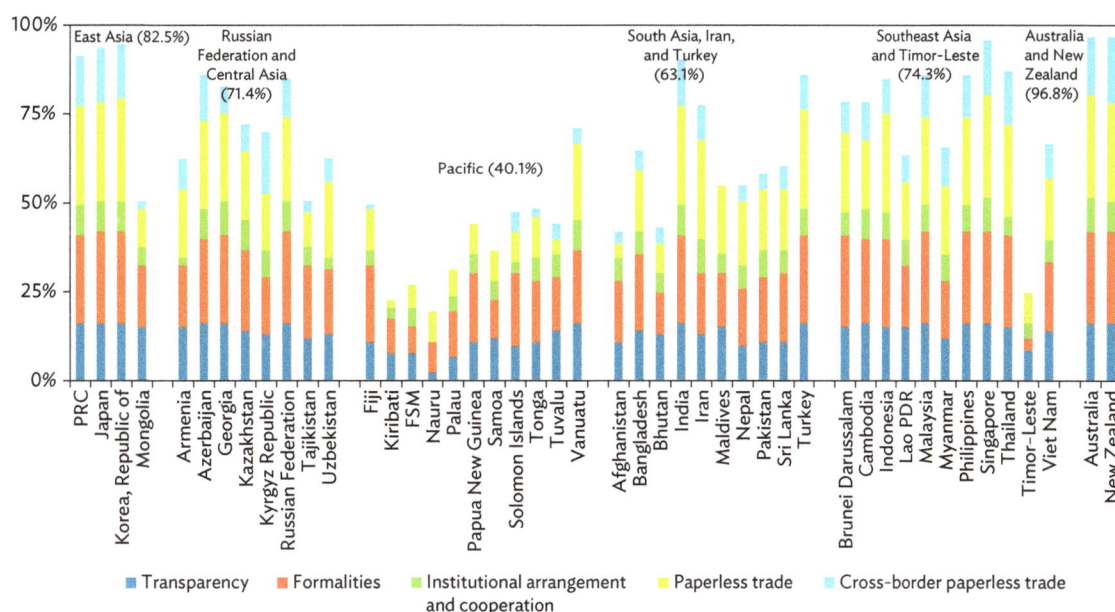

FSM = Federated States of Micronesia, Lao PDR = Lao People's Democratic Republic, PRC = People's Republic of China.

Note: Among the 58 measures surveyed across the United Nations regional commissions, three measures including *electronic submission of sea cargo manifests, alignment of working days and hours with neighboring countries at border crossings,* and *alignment of formalities and procedures with neighboring countries at border crossings* are excluded when calculating the overall score as they are not relevant to all countries surveyed. Four *transit facilitation* measures are also excluded for the same reason. Additionally, *sustainable trade facilitation* and *other trade facilitation* are excluded as these newly added groups of measures were not included in the earlier surveys, for comparison.

Source: UN Global Survey on Digital and Sustainable Trade Facilitation. untfsurvey.org.

**Figure 2:** Trade Facilitation Implementation in Asia and Pacific Subregions and Countries with Special Needs

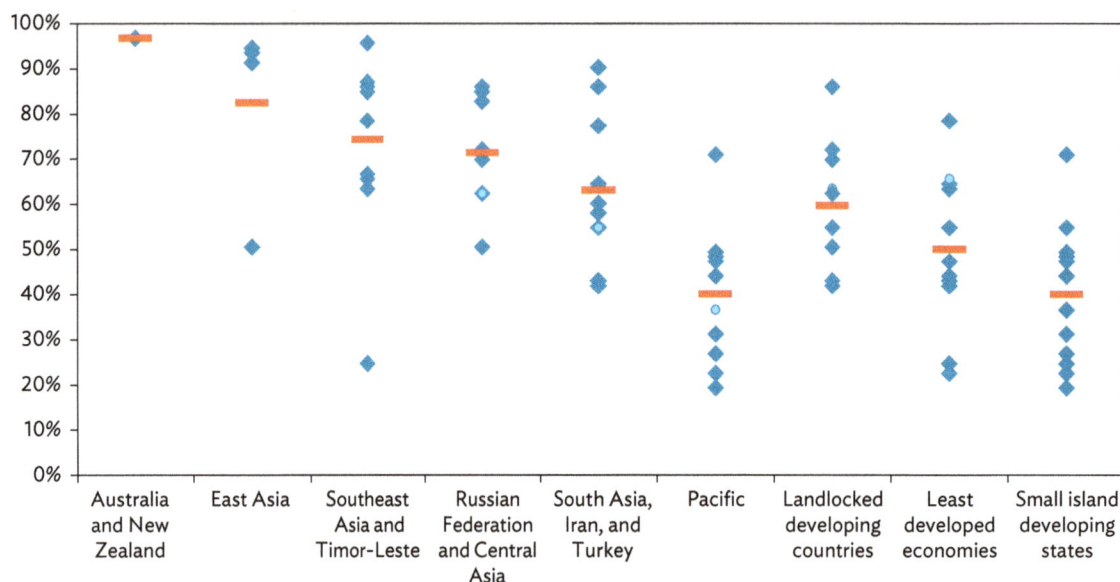

Note: Blue diamonds represent country scores; red lines are group averages.
Source: UN Global Survey on Digital and Sustainable Trade Facilitation. untfsurvey.org.

Within each subregional grouping, trade facilitation implementation differs substantially. Among the Pacific islands, differences in trade facilitation implementation levels are particularly evident. Trade facilitation implementation rates range from about 20% to 50%, with the exception of Vanuatu, which had a score of over 70%. This may be because these island economies are geographically isolated and confront several restrictions and distinctive disadvantages toward trade facilitation under different conditions. The countries in the Pacific region face several challenges, including in critical capacity building, particularly in cross-border paperless trade.[5]

Differences are also evident in Southeast Asia and Timor-Leste, but are much less pronounced if Timor-Leste, a non-ASEAN country, is excluded from calculation. ASEAN regional integration efforts and the establishment of the ASEAN Single Window have fostered substantial progress on implementation of trade facilitation. The Southeast Asian subregion has outperformed numerous other subregions in implementation.

In general, countries with special needs have difficulty implementing trade facilitation measures, particularly *paperless trade* and *cross-border paperless trade* (Figure 2). The most vulnerable countries—landlocked developing countries, least developed countries, and small island developing states—encounter a variety of connection hurdles. The least developed countries are the world's poorest and most vulnerable.

---

[5]    The 2021 survey shows Pacific subregional implementation rate for *cross-border paperless trade* at only 8.08%.

As such, WTO rules, including TFAs, provide preferential treatment and flexibility. Meanwhile, landlocked developing countries, lacking access to the sea, and small island developing states, isolated as they are, face considerably higher communication and logistics costs.

In comparison to least developed countries or small island developing states, landlocked developing countries appear to have attained greater trade facilitation. This might be explained by the coordinated and continued efforts on trade facilitation matters under the Vienna Programme of Action. Most landlocked developing countries in Asia are also members of the Central Asia Regional Economic Cooperation program and as such benefit from joint efforts on customs modernization and cooperation efforts. Trade facilitation initiatives in the program offer technical assistance for the continuation of customs reforms and to improve the flow of goods within the region.

Various measures in *transparency* and *formality* are well implemented throughout the region. The *transparency* measure (which includes measures like advance publication/notification of new trade-related regulations before their implementation, publication of existing import–export regulations on the internet, and stakeholder consultation on new draft regulations) has been the most widely implemented. The *formalities* and *transit facilitation* measures have reached implementation rates of over 75%. The *institutional arrangements and collaboration* measures reached average implementation of 68% in the region.

For *digital trade facilitation* measures, the regional average implementation of the *paperless trade* measures stands at 62.4%. While many economies have developed legislative frameworks to promote *paperless trade*, average adoption does not exceed 40%. Many developing countries have still low implementation for many measures under the *cross-border paperless trade*.

To reflect the Sustainable Development Goals covering trade facilitation, the *sustainable trade facilitation* group has been included since the 2017 survey. Among these sustainable trade facilitation measures, *agricultural trade facilitation* has been well-implemented (Figure 3). For other measures in the *sustainable trade facilitation* group, few countries have tailored efforts to help SMEs and women, as seen by the low average implementation rates of 41.7 % and 33.3 % for *trade facilitation for SMEs* and *women in trade facilitation*.

Digital trade transformation can support sustainable and development-focused benefits by lowering barriers. Figure 4 illustrates the high positive correlation between digital and sustainable dimensions of trade facilitation. The regional average implementation rates for *digital* and *sustainable* groups are 58% and 55%, respectively. Countries achieving higher implementation of the *digital trade facilitation* group have generally also performed well on the *sustainable trade facilitation* group. Overall, more advanced countries have performed better in both digital and sustainable dimensions than less advanced countries. The PRC, India, and the Republic of Korea are among the best performers in *sustainable trade facilitation*, while Australia and New Zealand are top performers in *digital trade facilitation*. Singapore has achieved over 90% for both groups.

**Figure 3:** Implementation of Groups of Trade Facilitation Measures, Asia and Pacific Average

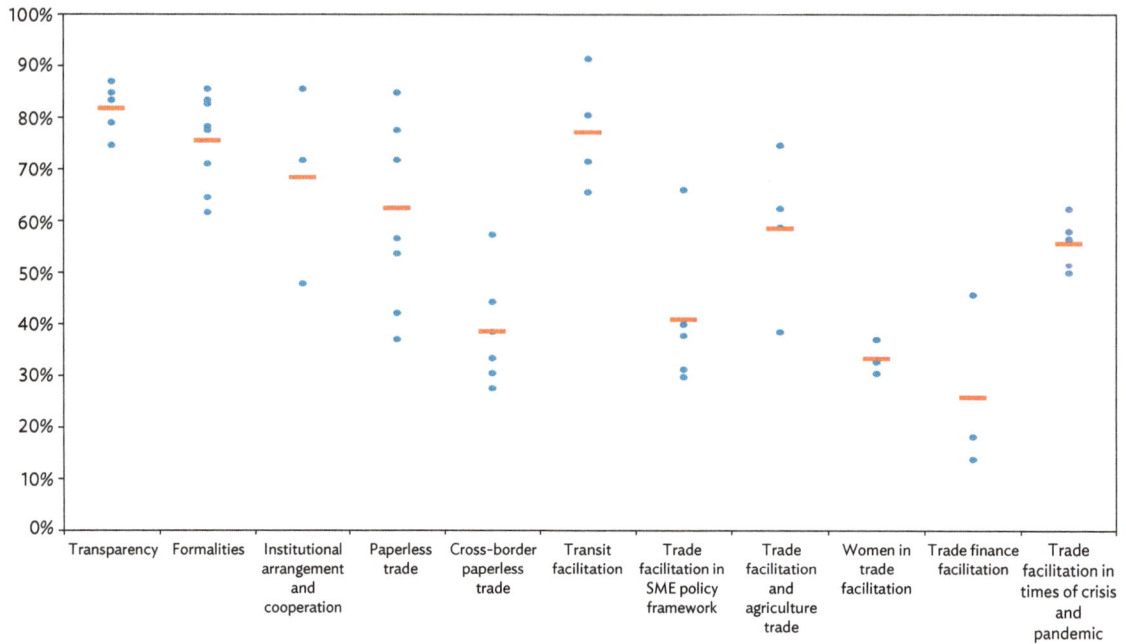

SMEs = small and medium-sized enterprises.

Note: Blue dots represent country scores; red lines are group averages.

Source: UN Global Survey on Digital and Sustainable Trade Facilitation. 2021. untfsurvey.org.

**Figure 4:** Implementation of Digital and Sustainable Dimensions of Trade Facilitation

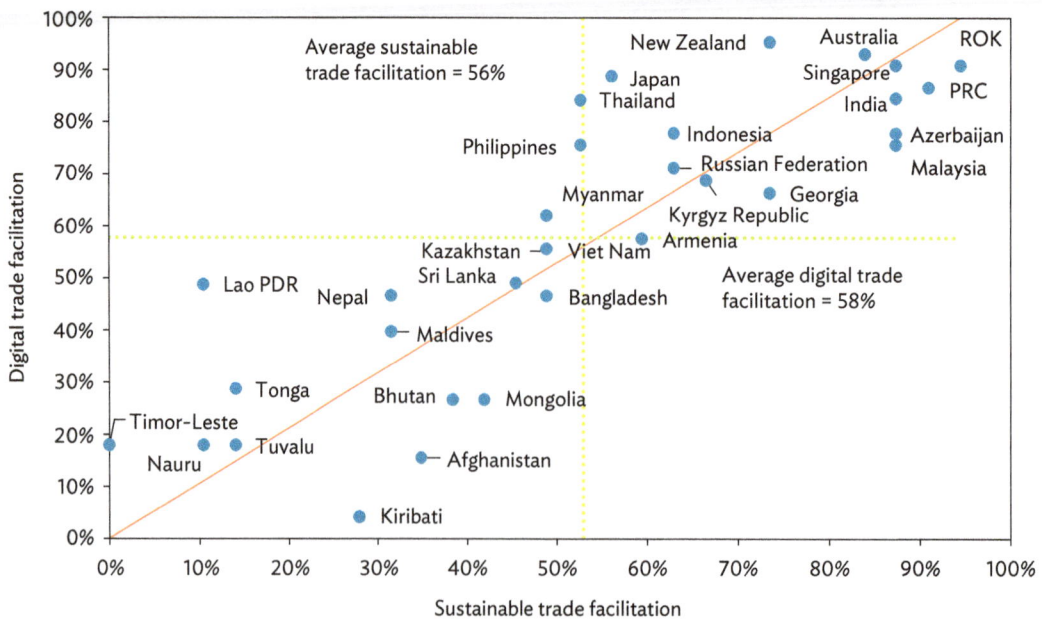

Lao PDR = Lao People's Democratic Republic, PRC = People's Republic of China, ROK= Republic of Korea.

Source: UN Global Survey on Digital and Sustainable Trade Facilitation. 2021. untfsurvey.org.

At 25.8% implementation, *trade finance facilitation* is the least implemented of all measures. This is at least partly because data for roughly 30% of the countries for measures under this specific subgroup could not be collected. The findings suggest substantial opportunity for improvement in this area, particularly on trade financing for SMEs to alleviate their financial limitations. Also notable is that trade facilitation experts and officials who provided or validated the survey are not familiar with trade finance. Traditional trade facilitation actors may see procedures related to financing, payment, and transactions as outside their scope of work. Integrating trade finance practices into trade facilitation activities, including bridging trade finance to single windows, deserves attention in the future trade facilitation work.

Amid the ongoing COVID-19 pandemic, and given the impact it has imposed on the global trade system, *trade facilitation in times of crisis* is newly added in the 2021 survey.[6] As a matter of fact, all trade facilitation measures already included in the survey including those related to enhancing transparency, simplifying and streamlining trade procedures, and supporting digital trade are of relevance to cope with the current crisis. Still, specific measures both to manage the current crisis and to support resilient post-pandemic recovery have been added. With a reasonably high implementation rate of 55.7%, it is relatively better implemented than others. This rate might be explained by governments, quick efforts to ensure rapid and seamless movement of essential goods. Specific measures such as *agency in place to manage trade facilitation in times of crises and emergencies* and *online publication of emergency TF measures* are well implemented.[7] However, long-term measures such as *utilizing national trade facilitation committees or similar bodies* to coordinate trade facilitation efforts during crisis, and planning of resource allocation for future crises beyond COVID-19 are implemented to a lesser extent and could be addressed to  enhance country preparedness in the region to minimize trade disruptions.

Table 3 shows the most and least implemented measures under each trade facilitation subgroups. *Stakeholder consultation on new draft regulations (prior to their finalization)* is the most implemented measure under *transparency*, with more than 95% of the countries in the region at least implementing this measure on pilot basis. *Advance ruling on tariff classification and origin of imported goods* is the least implemented measure under *transparency*. Nonetheless, it has already been fully implemented in 52.2% of countries and implemented at least on a pilot basis by 89.1% of the countries.

*Separation of release from final determination of customs duties, taxes, fees, and charges* is the most implemented measure under *formalities* , with over 97% of countries in the region implementing the measure to some extent and 59% of the countries fully implementing it. In contrast, *establishment and publication of average release times* is the least implemented measure in the group, suggesting room for improvement in continuous and consistent time release studies in the region.

---

[6]    A survey on trade facilitation in times of crisis and pandemic was pilot tested in Asia and the Pacific and was further developed as a module in the 2021 Global Survey. See ESCAP (2021a).

[7]    For more information on trade facilitation good practices, see ESCAP (2021b).

**Table 3:  Most and Least Implemented Measures in Asia and the Pacific**

| Category | Most Implemented (% of countries) | | Least Implemented (% of countries) | |
|---|---|---|---|---|
| | Measure | Implemented Fully, Partially and on a Pilot Basis (%)/Full Implementation (%) | Measure | Implemented Fully, Partially and on a Pilot Basis (%)/Full Implementation (%) |
| Transparency | Stakeholders' consultation on new draft regulations (prior to their finalization) | 95.7/69.6 | Advance ruling on tariff classification and origin of imported goods | 89.1/52.2 |
| Formalities | Separation of release from final determination of customs duties, taxes, fees, and charges | 97.8/58.7 | Establishment and publication of average release times | 84.8/41.3 |
| Institutional arrangement and cooperation | National legislative framework and/or institutional arrangements for border agencies' cooperation | 95.7/28.3 | Government agencies delegating border controls to customs authorities | 67.4/17.4 |
| Paperless trade | Automated customs system | 95.7/63.0 | Electronic application for customs refunds | 45.7/21.7 |
| Cross-border paperless trade | Laws and regulations for electronic transactions | 78.3/21.7 | Paperless collection of payment from a documentary letter of credit | 41.3/13.0 |
| Transit facilitation | Cooperation between agencies of countries involved in transit | 63.0/30.4 | Transit facilitation agreement(s) | 56.5/15.2 |
| Trade facilitation in SME policy framework | Trade-related information measures for SMEs | 84.8/37.0 | SMEs access single window | 43.5/13.0 |
| Trade facilitation and agriculture trade | Special treatment for perishable goods | 91.3/47.8 | Electronic application and issuance of SPS certificates | 56.5/15.2 |
| Women in trade facilitation | Women membership in the National Trade Facilitation Committee or similar bodies | 58.7/8.7 | TF policy/strategy to increase women's participation in trade | 45.7/8.7 |
| Trade finance facilitation | Variety of trade finance services available | 67.4/15.2 | Single window facilitates traders' access to finance | 21.7/4.3 |
| Trade facilitation in times of crisis | Coordination between countries on emergency trade facilitation measures | 87.0/26.1 | Plan in place to facilitate trade during future crises | 69.6/21.7 |

SMEs = small and medium-sized enterprises, SPS = sanitary and phytosanitary, TF = trade facilitation.

Source: UN Global Survey on Digital and Sustainable Trade Facilitation. untfsurvey.org.

Within *institutional arrangement and cooperation, national legislative framework and/or institutional arrangements for border agencies cooperation* is the most implemented measure, with over 95% of the countries implementing the measure to a certain extent. Nevertheless, only 28.3% of countries have fully implemented the measure.

Under *paperless trade, automated customs system* is the most implemented measure, with 63% of countries fully doing so and over 95% of countries at least partially implementing it. However, implementation of most other measures in the region, including the *electronic application for customs refunds*, are below the overall regional implementation average. This is a continuing trend, consistent with results from the previous survey.

*Cross-border paperless trade* is among the least implemented of all measures. It is promising that more than 78% of countries have at least partially developed laws and regulations for electronic transactions. However, as identified by several readiness assessment studies, quite often notable gaps exist in their coverage; rigid provisions were also identified, as were inconsistencies between different legislations, suggesting the need for continued effort to modernize and harmonize legal and regulatory frameworks.[8] With a lack of relevant laws and regulations, or gaps in them, among the reasons, *paperless collection of payment from a documentary letter of credit* is the least implemented measure, with only about 41% of the countries at least partially implementing and only 13% fully implementing.

When it comes to the *sustainable trade facilitation* group, measures under the *agricultural trade facilitation* have been comparatively well implemented, with *special treatment for perishable goods* in the lead. Measures targeting SMEs and women are implemented to a lesser extent. *Trade-related information measures for SMEs* is the most implemented measure under the subgroup, with 85% of countries implemented. On the other hand, *SMEs access single window* is the least implemented measure under this subgroup, with only 56% of countries in the region implementing it to some extent, and full implementation in only 13%. *Women's membership in the national trade facilitation committee or similar bodies* is the most implemented measure under *women in trade facilitation*, and *trade facilitation policy/strategy to increase women's participation in trade* is the least implemented.

## 1.2.2   Progress in Implementation from 2019 to 2021

In Asia and the Pacific, survey results show progress during 2019 and 2021, when the third and fourth survey results are compared. Overall, average implementation for 31 common trade facilitation measures increased from 58.9% in 2019 to 64.9% in 2021 (Figure 5). The pace of the rise in implementation declined from 2019 to 2021, after a 10-percentage-point increase between 2017 and 2019. Part of the reason for the slowdown is COVID-19 and associated barriers in global trade, with many countries implementing import and export restrictions since the pandemic started. Further, countries such as Australia, the Republic of Korea, New Zealand, and Singapore already have high implementation, exceeding 90%

---

[8]    Readiness assessment for cross-border paperless trade country reports are available in ESCAP (2020).

**Figure 5:** Trade Facilitation Implementation by Subregion, 2019 and 2021

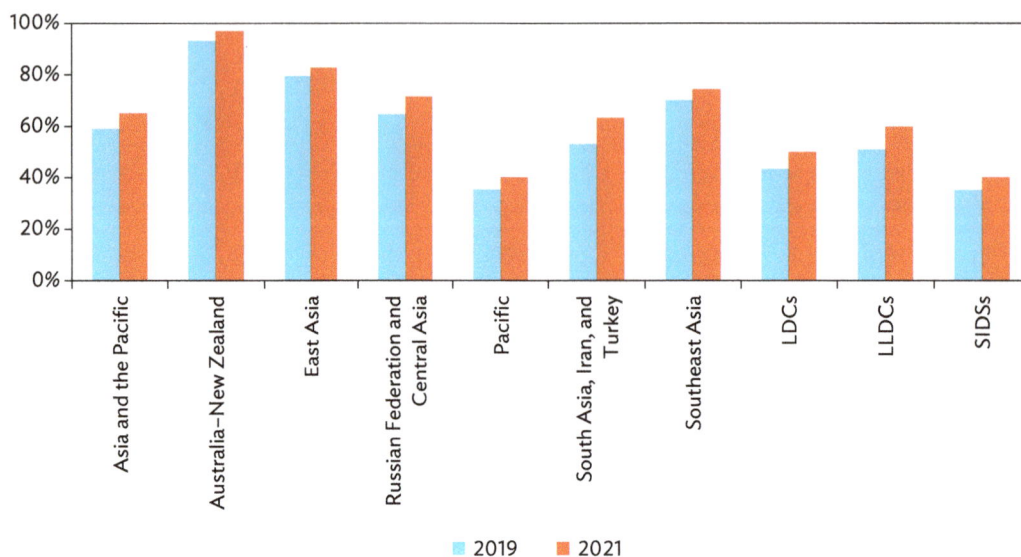

LDC = least developed country, LLDC = landlocked developing country, SIDS = small island developing state.
Source: UN Global Survey on Digital and Sustainable Trade Facilitation. untfsurvey.org.

in the 2019 survey, limiting further potential. Nonetheless, the growth rate is still positive following the trends of prior surveys (a 5.6 percentage point rise between 2015 and 2017), indicating a steady upward trend. South Asia, Iran, and Turkey have made the most improvement, with the subregion's implementation rate increasing from 53.1% in 2019 to 63.1% in 2021. The Russian Federation and Central Asia has also made significant progress, with the subregion's implementation rate increasing 6.9 percentage points. Similarly, the Pacific islands have made substantial progress, as shown by a 4.9 percentage point rise in their implementation rate, to 40.1% in 2021. Given the significant challenges in the Pacific from COVID-19, including evaporation of tourists, significant interruptions to international commerce, and a decline in remittances, this improvement is even more significant and meaningful.

Over the past 2 years, the most progress was in implementation of *cross-border paperless trade*, with the overall implementation rate increasing from 31.2% in 2019 to 38.5% in 2021. *Paperless trade* implementation also increased 5.7 percentage points. With the implementation of compatible, integrated, and synchronized bilateral, subregional, and regional platforms—as well as acceleration of digital transformation triggered by COVID-19—countries in the region have strived to improve digital infrastructure to facilitate trusted and secure data sharing. This is reflected in the survey results. WTO-TFA-related metrics, such as *institutional arrangement and cooperation, transparency,* and *formalities* have also strengthened, with increments of 5.7, 5.1, and 5.4 between 2019 and 2021, respectively. *Transparency* and *formalities* were the two most implemented (over 75%) in 2019, and the progress made over the last 2 years is comparatively less pronounced (Figure 6).

**Figure 6:  Implementation of Groups of Trade Facilitation Measures in Asia and the Pacific, 2019 and 2021**

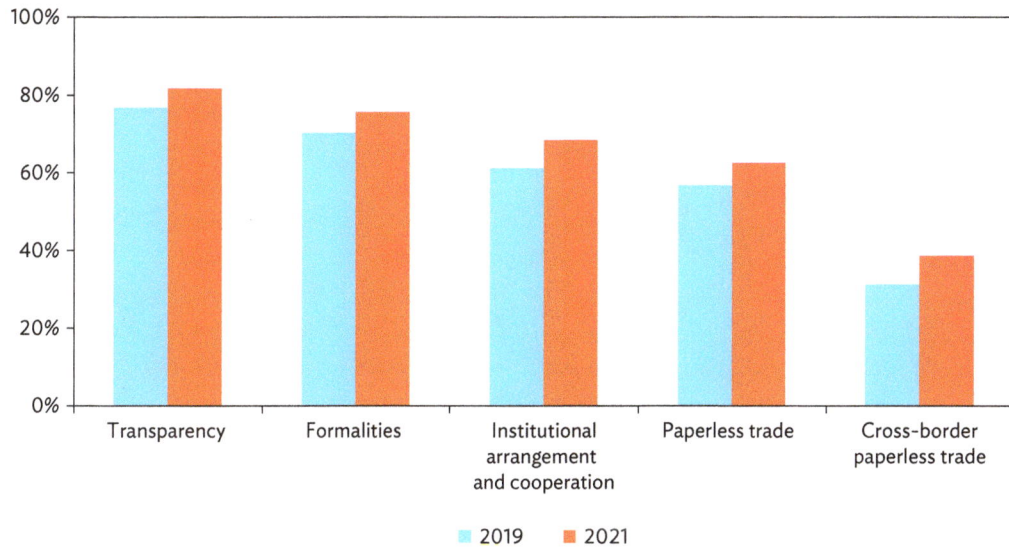

Source: UN Global Survey on Digital and Sustainable Trade Facilitation. untfsurvey.org.

# 2 Impact of Trade Facilitation on Trade Costs

To quantify trade facilitation impact on trade costs to economies, this chapter applies a trade cost model to examine trade cost changes as a result of improved trade facilitation and trade infrastructure, such as port connectivity and access to credit.

## 2.1 | Model and Data

Components of trade costs, referring to Arvis et al. (2016), can be distinguished into several factors, such as a geographic factor (distance, adjacency of countries, and "landlockedness"), cultural distance (common official/unofficial language, colonial relationships, having a common colonizer, and formerly same country), presence of trade policies (regional trade agreements or tariffs), prevalence of decent soft infrastructure (access to finance), and hard infrastructure (liner shipping connectivity [LSCI] for trade. In addition, trade facilitation implementation can be thought of as a factor affecting trade cost. Accordingly, specification of the trade cost model is as follows:

$$\ln(\tau_{ij}) = \beta_0 + \beta_1 \ln(gtariff_{ij}) + \beta_2 \ln(dist_{ij}) + \beta_3 (contig_{ij}) + \beta_4 (comlang\_off_{ij})$$
$$+ \beta_5 (comlang\_ethno_{ij}) + \beta_6 (colony_{ij}) + \beta_8 (comcol_{ij}) + \beta_8 (smctry_{ij}) + \beta_8 (rta_{ij})$$
$$+ \beta_{10} (landlocked_{ij}) + \beta_{11} \ln(credit_i) + \beta_{12} \ln(LSCI_i) + \beta_{13} \ln(TF_i) + D_j + \varepsilon_{ij}$$

Table 4 summarizes variable definitions, data treatment, data sources, and expected signs of trade cost factors. Trade facilitation implementation is computed based on 31 general and digital trade facilitation measures in the fourth Global Survey.[9] The model also includes partner fixed effect ($D_j$) and robust and clustered standard errors by country pair to take care of cross-country heterogeneity. The model is estimated across a cross-section of 115 reporting countries using ordinary least squares.

---

[9] Survey data for 2019 were updated based on the information collected in 2021. Some economies whose data were available in 2019 but not in 2021 are included with the assumption that level of trade facilitation implementation is unchanged. This is to ensure that it corresponds with data from the ESCAP-World Bank trade cost database, of which the latest data year is 2017–2019.

**Table 4:  Data Source, Definition, Treatment, Source, and Expected Sign**

| Variable | Definition | Data Treatment | Source | Expected Sign |
|---|---|---|---|---|
| $\tau_{ij}$ | Comprehensive trade costs. | Average of 2017–2019 | World Bank–ESCAP Trade Cost Database | |
| $gtariff_{ij}$ | Geometric average tariff factor (1+rate) that each reporting country (i) charges to its trade partner (j) and vice versa, which can be expressed by $$gtariff_{ijt} = \sqrt{tariff_{ijt} \times tariff_{ijt}}$$ | Average of 2017–2019 | World Integrated Trade Solution | + |
| $dist_{ij}$ | Geographic distance between country i and j. | … | CEPII | + |
| $contig_{ij}$ | Dummy variable of contiguity equal to 1 if country i and j share a common border and zero otherwise. | … | CEPII | – |
| $comlang\_off_{ij}$ | Dummy variable of common official language equal to 1 if country i and j use the same common official language and zero otherwise. | … | CEPII | – |
| $comlang\_ethno_{ij}$ | Dummy variable of common language equal to 1 if a language is spoken by at least 9% of the population in both countries and zero otherwise. | … | CEPII | – |
| $colony_{ij}$ | Dummy variable equal to 1 if country i and j were ever in colonial relationship and zero otherwise. | … | CEPII | – |
| $comcol_{ij}$ | Dummy variable equal to 1 if country i and j had a common colonizer after 1945 and zero otherwise. | … | CEPII | – |
| $smctry_{ij}$ | Dummy variable equal to 1 if country i and j were or are the same country and zero otherwise. | … | CEPII | – |
| $rta_{ij}$ | Dummy variable equal to 1 if country i and j are members of the same regional trade agreement and zero otherwise. | Latest definition in 2019 | Egger and Larch (2008) | – |
| $landlocked_{ij}$ | Dummy variable equal to 1 if either country i or j is landlocked and zero otherwise. | … | CEPII | + |
| $credit_{i}$ | Average access to credit index of country i.[a] | 0.0001 replacement/ average DB2018– DB2020 | Distance to frontier in Doing Business | – |
| $LSCI_{i}$ | Average scores of liner shipping connectivity index of country i. | Data gaps filled/average 2017–2019 | UNCTAD | – |
| $TFI_{i}$ | Percentage of TF implementation of country i, modeled as: (a) overall TF (tfi_i); or (b) general TF (generaltf_i) + digital TF (pxbptf_i). | 0.0001 replacement/ survey data 2019 with 2017 replacement if data are not available | Global Survey on Trade Facilitation and Paperless Trade Implementation: 2019 | – |

… = not applicable, CEPII = Le Centre d'Études Prospectives et d'Informations Internationales, ESCAP = Economic and Social Commission for Asia and the Pacific, UNCTAD = United Nations Conference on Trade and Development.

[a] Data for access to credit from the Doing Business Report are lagged 1 year, i.e., data from the Doing Business Report 2018 are from 2017.

Note: Where available, the average of the most recent data from 2017 onward is used in the estimation. Percentage of trade facilitation implementation of 2019 is used as trade cost data are up to 2019. The study assumes that implementation is at the level of 2017 if those economies do not submit data for 2019. Data filling for liner shipping connectivity is required to ensure inclusion of landlocked economies. Port countries are used as proxies for landlocked countries' portal performance. For the trade facilitation components and credit information index, zeros are replaced by 0.0001 to prevent observations from being omitted in the estimation. The lists of countries included in the analysis are presented in the annexes.

Source: ESCAP.

## 2.2 | Empirical Results

Table 5 shows results of estimates from the trade cost model. The model is distinguished into two main trade facilitation specifications: model (1) estimates overall trade facilitation implementation based on 31 main trade facilitation measures; and model (2) segregates effects into two groups of trade facilitation measures defined in Table 4—general trade facilitation (*transparency, formality and institutional arrangement and cooperation measures*) and digital trade facilitation (*paperless and cross-border paperless trade measures*).

The results of trade policies (tariffs and regional trade agreements), soft and hard infrastructure (access to finance and liner shipping connectivity), as well as a trade facilitation factor, are all statistically significant with expected impact on trade costs. The impact of tariff reduction on trade cost remains crucial and effective even though efforts in tariff reduction have been encouraged in the past 10 years. Table 5 shows that a 10% change in tariff leads to a reduction of trade costs by almost 7%, on average. A 10% improvement of overall trade facilitation implementation results in about a 3% reduction in trade costs. The models suggest that such a reduction is three times the trade cost reduction compared with the effect of a 10% improvement in hard infrastructure, such as maritime connectivity (1%).

## 2.3 | A Counterfactual Analysis

**Table 5:** Trade Cost Model Results

| Dependent Variable: $\ln\_\tau_{ij}$ | Beta Coefficient | | Standardized Beta | |
| --- | --- | --- | --- | --- |
| | (1) Overall Trade Facilitation (TF) | (2) General TF/ Digital TF | (1) Overall Trade Facilitation (TF) | (2) General TF/ Digital TF |
| ln_gtariff | 0.699*** [9.593] | 0.695*** [9.582] | 0.0877*** [9.593] | 0.0872*** [9.582] |
| ln_dist | 0.200***· [47.33] | 0.202*** [47.82] | 0.399*** [47.33] | 0.404*** [47.82] |
| contig | −0.108*** [−5.991] | −0.104*** [−5.755] | −0.0447*** [−5.991] | −0.0430*** [−5.755] |
| comlang_off | −0.0484*** [−3.718] | −0.0525*** [−3.983] | −0.0402*** [−3.718] | −0.0436*** [−3.983] |
| comlang_ethno | −0.0142 [−1.145] | −0.0105 [−0.841] | −0.0119 [−1.145] | −0.00883 [−0.841] |
| colony | −0.167*** [−10.08] | −0.168*** [−10.22] | −0.0588*** [−10.08] | −0.0591*** [−10.22] |
| comcol | −0.0533*** [−4.577] | −0.0518*** [−4.481] | −0.0344*** [−4.577] | −0.0334*** [−4.481] |
| smctry | −0.0748*** [−2.622] | −0.0573** [−2.040] | −0.0189*** [−2.622] | −0.0145** [−2.040] |
| landlocked_ij | 0.182*** [18.16] | 0.165*** [16.36] | 0.203*** [18.16] | 0.183*** [16.36] |

*continued next page*

**Table 5:** *Continued*

| Dependent Variable: $\ln\_\tau_{ij}$ | Beta Coefficient | | Standardized Beta | |
| --- | --- | --- | --- | --- |
| | (1) Overall Trade Facilitation (TF) | (2) General TF/ Digital TF | (1) Overall Trade Facilitation (TF) | (2) General TF/ Digital TF |
| rta | −0.0871*** [−12.86] | −0.0883*** [−13.15] | −0.101*** [−12.86] | −0.102*** [−13.15] |
| ln_credit_i | −0.0135* [−1.759] | −0.00591 [−0.743] | −0.0124* [−1.759] | −0.00546 [−0.743] |
| ln_lsci_i | −0.101*** [−28.83] | −0.103*** [−30.05] | −0.225*** [−28.83] | −0.229*** [−30.05] |
| ln_tfi_i | −0.304*** [−25.52] | | −0.224*** [−25.52] | |
| ln_generaltf_i | | −0.0694*** [−5.288] | | −0.0486*** [−5.288] |
| ln_pxbptf_i | | −0.192*** [−19.99] | | −0.201*** [−19.99] |
| Constant | 1.477*** [12.93] | 1.042*** [9.019] | | |
| Observations | 10,836 | 10,836 | 10,836 | 10,836 |
| R-squared | 0.594 | 0.597 | 0.594 | 0.597 |
| Reporter fixed effects | No | No | No | No |
| Partner fixed effects | Yes | Yes | Yes | Yes |
| Adjusted R-squared | 0.588 | 0.591 | 0.588 | 0.591 |

Note:  Regression estimates of Equation [1] use data specified in Table 4.

*** $p<0.01$, ** $p<0.05$, and * $p<0.1$; t-stats in square parentheses.

Source: Authors' calculations.

Further questions arise about what the magnitude of trade cost reduction will be when a country improves a set of trade facilitation measures. This study conducts counterfactual simulations to identify the potential effects of three "cases" of trade facilitation measures in trade cost reduction across countries as follows:

- Case 1: Binding measures under the WTO TFA

- Case 2: Binding and nonbinding measures under the WTO TFA

- Case 3: Binding and nonbinding measures under the WTO TFA, together with digital trade facilitation measures not integrated in the WTO TFA (WTO TFA+)

The following two scenarios are considered for each case:

- Scenario 1: Partially implemented trade facilitation measures in each case. All countries whose trade facilitation measures are either not implemented or are implemented on a pilot basis take action to achieve at least partial implementation.

- Scenario 2: Fully implemented trade facilitation measures in each case. All countries whose trade facilitation measures have not achieved full implementation take action to achieve full implementation.

Table 6 shows simulation results for Asia and Pacific economies. Partially implementing only binding measures results in less than a 2% trade cost reduction, while full implementation of only binding measures gives at best a 4% reduction in trade costs. A more ambitious result from full implementation of both binding and nonbinding measures shows at least a 7% decrease in trade costs. Under a WTO TFA+ case where digital trade facilitation measures not included in the WTO TFA are additionally implemented, the average trade cost reduction across countries increases to more than 13% in case of full implementation.

Table 6 also illustrates the average reduction of trade costs in Asia and the Pacific associated with two different groups of trade facilitation measures, i.e., general trade facilitation measures and digital trade facilitation measures. Both scenarios of partial and full implementation indicate that the largest trade cost reduction is from partial or full implementation of paperless and cross-border paperless trade measures, which goes beyond what is required in the WTO TFA.

**Table 6:** Changes in International Trade Costs of Asia and the Pacific as a Result of World Trade Organization Trade Facilitation Agreement Implementation

| Trade Costs Model | WTO TFA (binding only) | | WTO TFA (binding + nonbinding) | | WTO TFA+ (binding + nonbinding + other paperless and cross-border paperless trade) | |
|---|---|---|---|---|---|---|
| | Partially Implemented | Fully Implemented | Partially Implemented | Fully Implemented | Partially Implemented | Fully Implemented |
| **Model 1** | | | | | | |
| Overall trade facilitation | −1.74% | −4.11% | −2.81% | −6.64% | −7.65% | −13.40% |
| **Model 2** | | | | | | |
| General trade facilitation measures | −0.56% | −1.36% | −0.73% | −1.91% | −0.92% | −2.18% |
| Digital trade facilitation measures | − | − | −1.56% | −2.80% | −8.78% | −13.09% |

− = no measures, WTO TFA = World Trade Organization Trade Facilitation Agreement.

Note: There are no digital trade facilitation measures that are classified as WTO TFA binding measures.

Source: Authors' calculations.

Country data show that reduction in trade costs from their WTO TFA implementation in many developing countries, especially ASEAN and East Asian countries, may be limited. This is because these countries have already implemented many binding and/or nonbinding measures under the WTO TFA, as indicated in their notifications to the WTO, even before the agreement was concluded in 2013. Also, some of these ASEAN and East Asian countries have accomplished certain measures of advanced WTO TFA/WTO TFA+ measures.

In further improving, countries should pursue digitalization of trade procedures and enable seamless electronic exchange of data and documents across countries. These efforts could include interoperability of single windows across countries/regions, blockchain technology, e-certificates for sanitary and phytosanitary, cross-border e-commerce law, related cross-border mobile applications, etc.

It is also worth identifying magnitudes of trade cost reductions associated with soft and hard trade-related infrastructural reforms at large, which may incorporate improvements in transport and other trade-related infrastructure and services.[10] Thus, the following two additional simulation scenarios were conducted using regression estimates:

- Scenario 3: Enhancement in maritime connectivity. Countries with liner shipping connectivity scores below the developing country average/high income (Organisation for Economic Co-operation and Development [OECD]) average take action to bring their scores to equivalent levels.

- Scenario 4: Enhancement in access to financing. Countries with access to credit scores below the developing country average/high income OECD average take action and bring their scores to equivalent levels.

**Table 7:** **Changes in Trade Cost of Asia and the Pacific from Better Port Connectivity and Trade Finance**

|  | Improve to Developing Economies' Average (model 1/model 2) | Improve to OECD Average (model 1/model 2) |
|---|---|---|
| Maritime connectivity | −3.36%/−3.42% | −6.12%/−6.22% |
| Access to finance | −0.16%/−0.07% | −0.28%/−0.12% |

OECD = Organisation for Economic Co-operation and Development.

Source: Authors' calculation.

As shown in Table 7, improvement of maritime connectivity, as in scenario 3, would reduce trade costs in Asia and the Pacific by 3% to 6%. Improvement of access to credit, as in scenario 4, could reduce trade costs by 0.1% to 0.3%. While they cannot be easily compared with the impacts presented earlier in the implementation of WTO TFA and paperless trade measures,[11] such reductions related to these two types of infrastructure are significant, signaling the benefits of developing a traditional approach to trade facilitation and trade transactional cost reduction.

---

[10]    See WTO *World Trade Report* 2015 for a recent and comprehensive discussion of trade facilitation definitions (WTO 2015).

[11]    Notably, these estimates are calculated using the same group of countries in earlier simulations; they include a significant number of Asia and Pacific developing countries which see no individual cost reductions under the scenarios, because their maritime connectivity and credit information systems are already at or above the developing economies' average (or even the high-income average in the case of access to credit). Country-level analysis shows trade cost reductions from improving maritime connectivity for below average countries are significantly larger than those from WTO TFA implementation.

# 3 Conclusion and Way Forward

The regional analysis of data from the 2021 Global Survey on Digital and Sustainable Trade Facilitation shows continued progress on streamlining trade procedures in Asia and the Pacific. Implementation of 31 general and digital trade facilitation measures in the region rose by 6 percentage points over the last 2 years, leaving the average implementation rate to stand at 64.9% in 2021. Progress is moderate compared with the 10 percentage point increase between 2017 and 2019. That said, given the COVID-19 pandemic and the subsequent supply chain disruptions, such progress is significant. With trade cost on the rise, especially a recent surge in shipping costs, continuous efforts in trade facilitation implementation could help bend the trend.

Most countries in the region are actively implementing measures in improving *transparency*, streamlining the *formalities*, and enhancing *institutional arrangement and cooperation mechanisms*. In addition, the pandemic has accelerated digital transformation. Countries in the region have strived to improve their digital infrastructure to enable paperless trade and facilitate trusted and secure data sharing among partners. At the time of writing this report, all ASEAN members have joined the ASEAN Single Window (ASW) Live Operation, which allowed the granting of preferential tariff treatment based on the ASEAN Trade in Goods Assessment e-Form D exchanged through the ASW.

However, implementation of *cross-border paperless trade* remains challenging, with a regional average implementation rate below 40%. Implementation of bilateral and subregional paperless trade systems remain mostly at the pilot stage.

The analysis presented, based on the latest data available, confirms that digital trade facilitation measures can result in significant benefits to the countries in the region. Full digital trade facilitation implementation beyond the WTO TFA could cut average trade cost in the region by over 13%, 7 percentage points more than what could be expected from implementation of the WTO TFA.

Moving forward, trade facilitation implementation may be seen as a step-by step process, based on the groups of measures included in the UN Global Survey (Figure 7). It begins with *enhancing the institutional arrangement* to develop and implement a trade facilitation strategy. The next step is to establish a *more transparent* trade process by making information available on existing regulations to all relevant stakeholders and ensuring these stakeholders are properly consulted when new regulations are being developed. Reducing inefficiencies or developing more efficient trade *formalities* follows. The reengineered processes could be implemented on paper-based existing procedures but, ultimately, can then be automated and developed into national *paperless trade systems*. The ultimate step is to enable trade data and documents within these systems, including national single windows, to be safely and securely used and reused by authorized stakeholders along the international supply chain. This will contribute to faster movement of goods and reduction of overall trade costs.[12]

---

[12]    This step-by-step process is inspired from and generally consistent with the UN/CEFACT step-by-step approach to trade facilitation toward a single window environment.

**Figure 7:** Moving Up the Trade Facilitation Ladder toward Seamless International Supply Chains

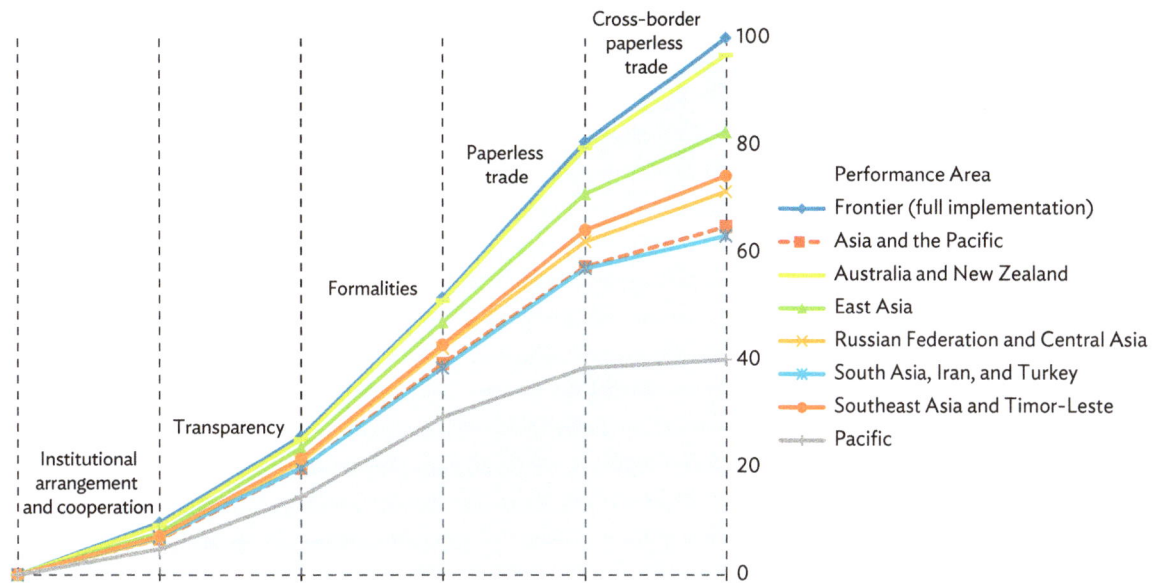

Note: The figure shows the cumulative trade facilitation implementation scores of Asia and Pacific subregions for 31 common trade facilitation measures included in the survey. Full implementation of all measures = 100.

Source: United Nations Global Survey on Digital and Sustainable Trade Facilitation. untfsurvey.org.

Actual implementation of all steps is in practice intertwined and long-term planning is important and essential to success. In particular for the last two steps, all countries need to work together to develop and implement the legal and technical protocols needed for the seamless exchange of regulatory and commercial data and documents within and between countries.

Fundamentally, it requires change in how trade is conducted, and it should be supported by high-level commitment and vision of the country's leadership to harnessing the benefits from trade digitalization. In this regard, the Framework Agreement on Facilitation of Cross-Border Paperless Trade in Asia and the Pacific could support countries to gradually move to "less-paper" and then to paperless and cross-border paperless trade by providing a dedicated and inclusive capacity-building–focused intergovernmental platform. All countries in the region are encouraged to become parties to the treaty as soon as possible in order to ensure that issues of their interest can be prioritized, including in terms of capacity building and technical assistance.

Sustainable trade facilitation is another indispensable dimension of trade facilitation. Implementation of inclusive measures to promote SMEs and the participation of women in trade remains low. SMEs represent a significant portion of the Asia and Pacific economy and workforce, yet trade facilitation measures tailored to SMEs are insufficient. These firms are still facing disproportionate barriers to trade due to inadequate access to digital infrastructure, insufficient information technology skills, and a lack of financial resources. This is particularly so during the COVID-19 pandemic. In this regard, building the capacity of SMEs in the trade facilitation regime is critical in achieving sustainable and inclusive development of economies in the region.

Similarly, efforts on gender mainstreaming in trade facilitation are lacking. Guiding women in understanding trade procedures, setting guidelines for standards bodies to ensure a more balanced representation of the interests of women and men, and promoting the participation and decision-making of women in trade facilitation and standards-related activities, could have a significant impact on increasing exports and enabling women to achieve higher income opportunities. High positive correlation between digital and sustainable dimensions of trade facilitation indicate the synergies that could be achieved by enhancing both dimensions. To this end, trade facilitation strategies should be designed inclusively.

The COVID-19 pandemic has exposed many weaknesses of the trading system.  The *trade facilitation in times of crisis* section of the survey shows that most governments in the region have swiftly implemented a number of short-term crisis measures to expedite movement of essential goods. Still, the implementation rate of crisis-related trade facilitation measures only stands at 55.7%, on average, essentially because many countries still lack long-term trade facilitation plans to enhance preparedness for future crises. It is imperative to enhance regional connectivity through coordinated trade facilitation actions at this pivotal time. Continued and sustained efforts should be made to further enhance cooperation, make trade information transparent, strengthen the capacity of countries to contribute to recovery, and prepare to adequately safeguard against future crises.

## REFERENCES

Arvis, J., Y. Duval, B. Shepherd, C. Utoktham, and A. Raj. 2016. Trade Costs in the Developing  World: 1996–2010. *World Trade Review*. 15 (3). pp. 451-474. https://www.cambridge.org/core/journals/world-trade-review/article/abs/trade-costs-in-the-developing-world-19962010/D0A95C6CF747B51FFF550B86A4C90E1C doi:10.1017/S147474561500052X.

Economic and Social Commission for Asia and the Pacific (ESCAP).  2020. Readiness Assessments for Cross-Border Paperless Trade. https://www.unescap.org/resources/readiness-assessments-cross-border-paperless-trade#.

ESCAP. 2021a. Framework Agreement on Facilitation of Cross-border Paperless Trade in Asia and the Pacific. https://www.unescap.org/kp/cpta.

———. 2021b. Trade Facilitation in Times of Crisis and Pandemic: Practices and Lessons from the Asia-Pacific Region. https://www.unescap.org/sites/default/d8files/knowledge-products/Regional%20report-Trade%20facilitation%20in%20times%20of%20crisis%20and%20pandemic_0.pdf.

———. 2021c. Digital and Sustainable Trade Facilitation in the Asia-Pacific: Regional Report 2021.

Egger, P. H., and M. Larch. 2008. Interdependent Preferential Trade Agreement Memberships: An Empirical Analysis. *Journal of International Economics*. 76(2). pp.384–399.

United Nations Conference on Trade and Development (UNCTAD). 2021a. Shipping during COVID-19: Why Container Freight Rates have Surged. https://unctad.org/news/shipping-during-covid-19-why-container-freight-rates-have-surged.

———. 2021b. How to Cushion Consumers from High Maritime Freight Rates. https://unctad.org/news/how-cushion-consumers-high-maritime-freight-rates.

World Trade Organization (WTO). 2015. *World Trade Report 2015*. Geneva. https://www.wto.org/english/res_e/booksp_e/world_trade_report15_e.pdf.

# SUPPLY CHAINS OF CRITICAL GOODS AMID THE COVID-19 PANDEMIC—DISRUPTIONS, RECOVERY, AND RESILIENCE

# 1 Introduction

In the last 2 decades, trade flows have risen as firms have fragmented production activities. As they have strived to lower costs and improve efficiency, they have divided single production processes into multiple components and activities, often spread across geographic locations beyond national boundaries. This resulted in complex supply chains driven by trade and investment liberalization, lower transport costs, and advances in logistics and communication technologies. Though external factors have disrupted supply chains from time to time, including disasters triggered by natural hazards, financial crises, and epidemics, they have also resiliently recovered from such disruptions.

The coronavirus disease (COVID-19) pandemic, as noted, put considerable strain on global supply chains. Rising infections and national lockdowns and isolation rules slowed or even temporarily stopped the flow of goods across borders. Border closures, export controls, and additional health and safety protocols for shippers disrupted the flow of goods. This clearly revealed supply chain vulnerabilities. Lack of diversification across suppliers or countries for critical raw materials stalled manufacturing, endangering many livelihoods. On the demand side, mobility restrictions and anxiety over unavailability of essential goods raised prices, leading countries to ban exports to meet domestic demand. Unlike the previous disruptions, which were localized and developed over time, the impact of COVID-19 has been unprecedented, affecting global trade and incomes in a short span of time.

More particularly, the pandemic significantly stressed medical goods supply and food availability, threatening people's health and well-being. While vaccines were developed at an unprecedented speed, deploying these to the global community, including Asia and the Pacific, has posed many challenges. Only a few countries are able to produce vaccines, trade restrictions and domestic stockpiling have challenged manufacturing at a global scale. Insufficient funding for adequate transport, logistics, and temperature-controlled storage infrastructure has hampered developing economies' access to vaccines. It was also a challenge to boost the production of personal protective equipment (PPE) such as face masks and respirators during the pandemic, as most global production was outsourced to the People's Republic of China (PRC) and lean inventory management systems across global supply chains could not respond quickly enough to surging global demand. Meanwhile, export bans and trade regulations challenged food trade, especially early in the pandemic, as major exporters of food staples such as wheat and rice imposed export restrictions, causing prices to spike in major importing countries. Mobility restrictions, lockdowns, and unavailability of transport also hampered domestic production of various food crops, including access to seeds and fertilizers, crop harvests, and distribution to urban centers. This also restricted port operations for distribution of imported food.

As the pandemic continued, addressing supply chain issues became crucial for the safe and quick delivery of goods and services. Governments across the globe made policy decisions to sustain business operations and improve availability of critical goods. They created fast-track lanes at border crossings, streamlined certification, relaxed regulation on trade in medical goods and food, and exempted related sectors from lockdown restrictions.

Discussions of supply chains will continue beyond the pandemic as countries resume their economic growth and revisit supply chain challenges and increase resiliency.

This theme chapter analyzes sources and impacts of previous disruptions and the current pandemic, the responses of firms and governments, and suggests policy for the way forward. Section 2 presents background on the sources of and responses to supply chain disruptions before and during the pandemic. The section also presents a framework on supply chain resilience, based on which, section 3 discusses areas of vulnerabilities and capabilities of supply chains for these essential goods. Section 4 presents case studies, looking at supply chains of essential commodities such as vaccines, PPE, and food heavily affected during the pandemic. Section 5 concludes with policy recommendations for greater resilience of cross-border supply chains.

# 2 Supply Chain Disruptions

## 2.1 | Causes of Disruptions

Supply chains have been disrupted to a greater or lesser extent by natural hazards such as typhoons, tsunamis, and earthquakes, as well as epidemic disease (Box 1). Table 1 lists major events that significantly disrupted supply chains and the estimated economic impacts. For example, the tsunami and nuclear fallout in 2011 in Japan affected automotive supply chains, with double-digit percentage declines in vehicle output in the PRC, Thailand, and the United States. Japan's industrial production and exports dropped 7% and 8%, respectively, during the second quarter of the year (Pau et al. 2018). During the flooding of Thailand's Chao Phraya river in 2011, many industrial parks were inundated, and the country's automobile production dropped over 60% in the fourth quarter of that year.

---

### Box 1: Disasters Triggered by Natural Hazards in Asia and the Pacific

In the past 2 decades, about 40% of disasters triggered by natural hazards have happened in Asia and the Pacific, with 44% in the Americas and Africa. Hydrological (floods) and meteorological (storms) are the most frequent disasters, consistent with the rest of the world. Among subregions, the top three are Southeast Asia, East Asia, and South Asia, with a combined 86% of total disasters experienced by these regions.

#### Distribution of Disasters by Region, 2000–2021

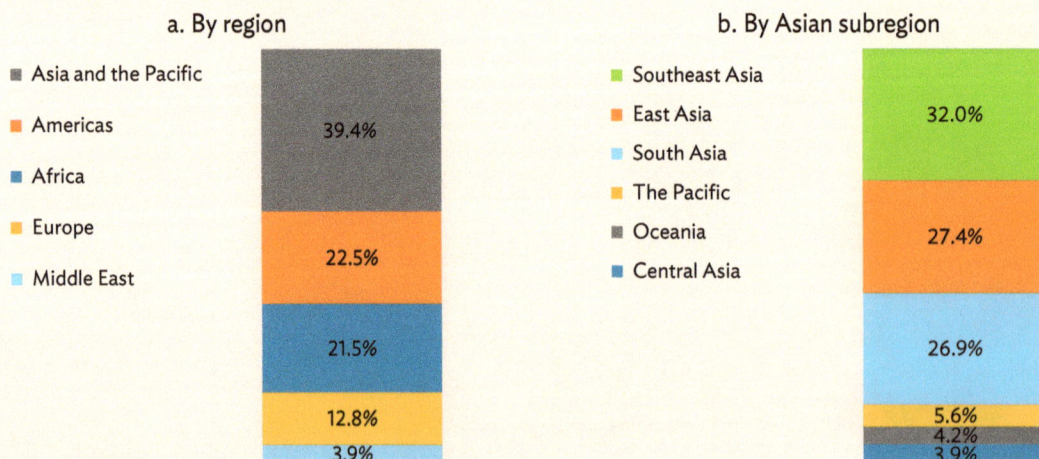

**a. By region**

- Asia and the Pacific — 39.4%
- Americas — 22.5%
- Africa — 21.5%
- Europe — 12.8%
- Middle East — 3.9%

**b. By Asian subregion**

- Southeast Asia — 32.0%
- East Asia — 27.4%
- South Asia — 26.9%
- The Pacific — 5.6%
- Oceania — 4.2%
- Central Asia — 3.9%

Notes: For an event to be considered a disaster, it must satisfy at least one of the following criteria: (i) 10 or more deaths, (ii) 100 or more people affected/injured/homeless, or (iii) official declaration of the country of a state of emergency and/or appeal for international assistance.

Source: Asian Development Bank calculations using the International Disaster Database. http://www.emdat.be (accessed June 2021).

---

## Table 1: Selected Supply Chain Disruptions

| Consequences/Damage | Post-Event Changes |
|---|---|
| **Disaster triggered by natural hazards** | |
| **Tohoku earthquake and tsunami—Japan, March 2011** | |
| • Power outages for months and some ports out of operation for more than a month.<br>• Almost 20,000 dead or missing with substantial destruction of physical capital.<br>• Economic damage around $210 billion.<br>• Manufacturing output fell 15% in March and did not recover until July.<br>• Japanese auto market share in the United States dropped from 40% in March to 30% in July and only repositioned back in 2012. | • Invested in accurate tsunami warning devices, installed seawalls and breakwaters.<br>• Raised stocks and inventory of parts, diversified production, and created alternative manufacturing capabilities.<br>• Opted for more standardized vehicle parts to improve efficiency and enable alternative production. |
| **Flood—Thailand, 2011** | |
| • 19,000 destroyed homes.<br>• 2.5 million displaced people/813 dead.<br>• 17,578 square kilometers of impacted farmlands.<br>• $46.5 billion of economic damages and losses ($32 billion in manufacturing sector).<br>• Reduced the world's industrial production by 2.5%. | • Redesigned their supply chain network to be more diversified in terms of location.<br>• The Government of Thailand established the National Catastrophe Insurance Fund of Thailand to create a Catastrophe Insurance Policy.<br>• Invested on infrastructure projects to mitigate flooding. |
| **Trade restriction** | |
| **2007–2008 food price crisis** | |
| • Export restrictions, panic buying of major rice-importing countries.<br>• World rice prices increased by 117% to 149% in the first quarter of 2008. | • ASEAN member countries establishing rice reserves, facilitating regional rice trade, food security information system, and innovations through research and development. |
| **Economic crisis** | |
| **2007–2008 financial crisis** | |
| • Around 67,000 factories in the PRC have gone bankrupt.<br>• 35% decrease in exports across Asia.<br>• Intra-Asia trade decreased 48% at the highest.<br>• Global trade decreased by two-thirds in 2009 from 2008. | • Refocused on stability and risk management but with less emphasis on cost reduction. |
| **Health crisis** | |
| **2003 Severe acute respiratory syndrome (SARS) outbreak** | |
| • 8,5000 infected / 912 deaths.<br>• Estimated GDP loss of $13 billion combined for the PRC; Singapore; Hong Kong, China; and Taipei,China.<br>• Overall economic cost 0.5%–1% of annual GDP across the Asia-Pacific Economic Cooperation economies.<br>• Loss in tourism, leisure, and transport: $8.5 billion in the PRC, $1.4 billion in Malaysia, and $1.3 billion in Hong Kong, China.<br>• Hong Kong, China experienced high unemployment up to 8.7% until the outbreak was contained. | • Short-term adjustments business continuity plans such as working from home, video conferencing, setting up operations at parallel sites, or shifting operations to other locations.<br>• There were no major changes in the supply chain. However, the travel bans and quarantine made firms consider diversifying their production rather than one big facility in a single location. |

*continued next page*

**Table 1** *Continued*

| Ebola 2014–2016 outbreak in West Africa | |
| --- | --- |
| • Agricultural production declined and cross-border trade decreased as restrictions on movements, goods, and services increased.<br><br>• 28,600 confirmed cases and 11,325 deaths by the end of the outbreak.<br><br>• Estimated to have cost of $4.3 billion total for countries affected.<br><br>• Investments in Guinea, Liberia, and Sierra Leone dramatically decreased. | • UNICEF identified issues in manufacturing capacities for PPEs from their supplier and swiftly decided to form new contracts with different suppliers to ramp up PPE production.<br><br>• UNICEF provided long-range forecasts and established long-term arrangements with different suppliers to solve bottlenecks in their PPE supplies. |
| **1918 Influenza pandemic (Spanish flu)** | |
| • Estimated about 500 million infected and at least 50 million dead around the world.<br><br>• In the typical country, real per capita GDP declined by 6% and private consumption by 8%.<br><br>• Countries that suffered a 2% average death rate are thought to have experienced an estimated 26% drop in real stock returns. | • Information not available. |

ASEAN = Association of Southeast Asian Nations, GDP= gross domestic product, PPE = personal protective equipment, PRC = People's Republic of China, UNICEF = United Nations Children's Fund.

Sources: Barro, Ursúa, Weng (2020); Bénassy-Quéré et al. (2009); Boehm, Flaaen, and Pandalai-Nayar (2019); CDC (2015); CDC (n.d.); CRED (2011); Goentzel (2015); Haraguchi and Lall (2015); Keat (2009); Koshimura and Shuto (2015); Kumar (2012); Leckcivilize (2012); Mefford (2009); Noy and Shields (2019); Rushton et al. (2005); Tajitsu (2016); Wailes et al. (2012).

Despite Asia and the Pacific's vulnerability to natural hazards, several disasters triggered by these hazards in the last 2 decades have caused only short-term supply shocks in the region. They have not reduced operational capacity of firms, and exports bounced back more quickly than expected (Anbumozhi 2020).

Economic and financial crises have also impacted supply chains. For instance, during the 1997 Asian financial crisis, lack of liquidity led to collapse of demand and rippled along value chains. Full recovery happened after a year or two as many companies were able to recover with support from the banking sector (Anbumozhi 2020). During the 2007–2008 global financial crisis, falling global demand was coupled with a drop in demand for intermediate goods destined for assembly in Japan, the PRC, and the Republic of Korea. Reliance on inputs from Southeast Asian countries such as Indonesia, Malaysia, Singapore, Thailand, and Viet Nam also caused negative export shocks to these economies.

Conversely, adverse events led to reforms to make systems more resilient by strengthening monitoring potential hazards and supply chains; diversifying/enhancing production channels and capacity; and supporting research and development and information systems. In Japan, the 2011 Tohoku earthquake and tsunami led to the installation of seawalls and breakwaters and investments in more accurate tsunami warning devices. Business firms increased the stocks and inventory of parts, developed alternative manufacturing capabilities, and diversified production. In response to the 2011 flood in Thailand, companies diversified the location of their supply chains, while the government invested in flood mitigation infrastructure. A food price spike in 2007 prompted the Association of Southeast Asian Nations (ASEAN) economies to devise a comprehensive framework on food security that included a regional emergency rice reserve, measures to facilitate trade, food security information system, and rice research and development. In response to the global financial crisis of 2008, global supply chains saw renewed focus on risk management and stability with reduced emphasis on cost reduction. Health crises such as the 2003 severe acute respiratory syndrome (SARS) outbreak also led firms to consider diversifying suppliers in multiple geographic areas.

Epidemics in the past disrupted supply chains and all major outbreaks—Ebola, SARS, Spanish flu—infected and killed people. Yet, the COVID-19 pandemic has had abrupt and far-reaching impacts globally (Box 2), while the economic impact of previous epidemics were localized or spread more slowly across countries. Border closures, lockdowns, quarantines, and other means to control the virus spread weakened demand and disrupted supply chains, resulting in an overall decline in global trade (ADB 2021a), and the adverse impacts have been felt in supply chains across Asia and the Pacific.

Not long after the onset of the pandemic, most economies implemented drastic lockdowns, and new virus variants and recurring waves have made governments cautious about relaxing lockdowns and mobility measures. Such measures have hurt trade, with increasing prices and declining volume. Pre-pandemic, freight spot rates for ocean container transport were relatively stable, but prices jumped and continued to increase in 2021 due to a shortage of shipping containers combined with rising demand for goods (Figure 1). The airline cargo and passenger travel, measured in kilometers, plunged in 2020 and are expected to recover only slowly in 2021 (Figure 2).

Disruptions to global supply chains reverberated to other economies in the supply chain. For example, in the PRC, the slump in demand in electronics and automobiles and declining corporate earnings of multinational enterprises weighed on production capacity and export-oriented investments. In Southeast Asia, major disruptions of production and supply chains in many industries were affected as lockdown measures led to factory stoppages. In the early phase of the pandemic, major automotive manufacturers such as Mazda, Mitsubishi, and Nissan temporarily ceased their production in Thailand, while Ford suspended production in Thailand and Viet Nam as well as Toyota in Indonesia and Thailand (UNCTAD 2020). Global-value-chain-intensive manufacturing sectors, such as electronics and apparel, were also disrupted by lockdowns in the PRC, affecting the flow of parts and components in other subregions. About 40%–60% of electronics components for factories in Indonesia, Thailand, and Viet Nam are sourced from the PRC, including 55% of inputs for apparel factories in Cambodia, Myanmar, and Viet Nam. In South Asia, India experienced automotive production disruptions from port congestion and shortages of parts (e.g., electrical, interiors, lighting, and braking components), where 27% of these are imported from the PRC (Ernst and Young 2020). Similarly, India's manufacturing capacity of electronic equipment—such as telecom products, information technology (IT) hardware, consumer electronics, medical electronics, industrial electronics, and automotive electronics—was hampered by the lack of imported raw materials and components from the PRC and other countries.

Policies also played a role in disrupting supply chains, particularly in food. In Central Asia, which relies heavily on primary goods trade such as agriculture and mining, transboundary food security problems were observed during the early phase of the pandemic. In March 2020, key exporters of food staples including

## Box 2:  How Is the COVID-19 Pandemic Different from Past Crises?

According to the World Health Organization, as of May 2021, 170 million people had been infected around the world, with 3.4 million deaths. Though most countries have been vaccinating their populations, new variants and recent surges suggest that the pandemic will not end in the coming months. The COVID-19 pandemic is different from past crises in the sheer scale of its global impact.

In the 20 years before the COVID-19 pandemic, the world had experienced only a few large-scale outbreaks, the largest of which is the Ebola outbreak of 2014–2016, with 28,600 confirmed cases and 11,325 deaths (CDC 2015) while it was contained in West Africa. The 2003 SARS outbreak infected 8,098 worldwide with 774 deaths as governments were quick to react to the outbreak (CDC 2017). All of these are dwarfed by the Spanish flu in 1918–1919 which infected an estimated 500 million people around the world, with at least 50 million deaths (CDC 2019).

For COVID-19, given the lockdowns implemented to control the spread of the virus, economic activity stopped for the majority of the world. But the full impact has not yet been determined given the many differences in how countries have handled the situation and when it will end. According to the April 2021 World Economic Outlook, the global economy shrank 3.3% in 2020 (IMF 2021). The decline is larger than the 1.8% decline of global output in 2009 after the 2008–2009 global financial crisis (Kose and Ohnsorge 2019).

Ebola, by contrast, cost an estimated $4.3 billion for affected countries (Goentzel 2015). Though it was short-lived, the SARS outbreak affected the Asia-Pacific Economic Cooperation economies in an estimated range of 0.5% to 1% of the annual gross domestic product (Noy and Shields 2019). The Spanish flu was estimated to have seen real per capita GDP decline 6% in affected countries.

On unemployment, the International Labour Organization (ILO 2021) estimates that 8.8% of global working hours were lost relative to the fourth quarter of 2019 due to the pandemic. This is four times greater than during the 2008–2009 financial crisis. This loss in working hours saw global unemployment rise 33 million, from a 1.1% to 6.5% global unemployment rate. During the Ebola outbreak, countries such as Liberia experienced a 40% decrease in employment (World Bank 2014). Hong Kong, China, which was one of the main locations of the SARS outbreak, experienced high unemployment up to 8.7% until it was over (Noy and Shields 2019).

The pandemic was widely considered as a temporary shock to economic growth with V-shaped recoveries (Kharas 2020). This is however not equal for all. With increasing unemployment and multiple lockdowns not all will be able to get back to pre-pandemic levels. This is felt especially by households pushed below the poverty line. The World Bank (2020b) estimated that COVID-19 pushed a total of 150 million people into extreme poverty in 2020 and 2021. That is, around 1.4% of the world's population will fall into extreme poverty. The 2008–2009 financial crisis was estimated to have pushed 130–155 million people into poverty (World Bank 2008), the same number as pushed into poverty by the pandemic. Ebola affected countries in similar ways: poverty in Guinea, Liberia, and Sierra Leone increased 2.25% to 17.6% from base levels during 2014–2015 (UNDG 2015).

Sources: CDC (2015), (2017), (2019); IMF (2021); Kose and Ohnsorge (2020); Goentzel (2015); Barro et al. (2020); ILO (2021); World Bank (2008), (2014), (2020b); Noy and Shields (2019); Kharas (2020); UNDG (2015).

**Figure 1:** Freightos Baltic Global Container Index ($)

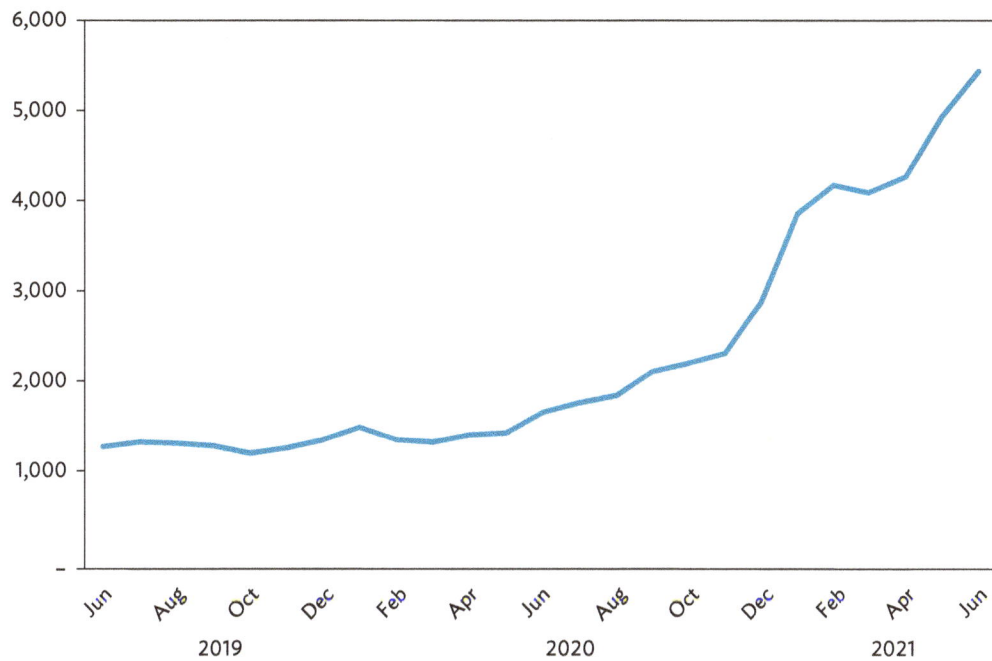

Note: This is a set of indexes that reflects ocean container transport spot freight rates across 12 global trade lanes.
Source: Freightos Baltic Index (FBX). Freightos Baltic Index (FBX): Global Container Freight Index. https://fbx.freightos.com/.

**Figure 2:** Global Passenger Kilometers and Cargo Tonne Kilometers (2019 = 100)

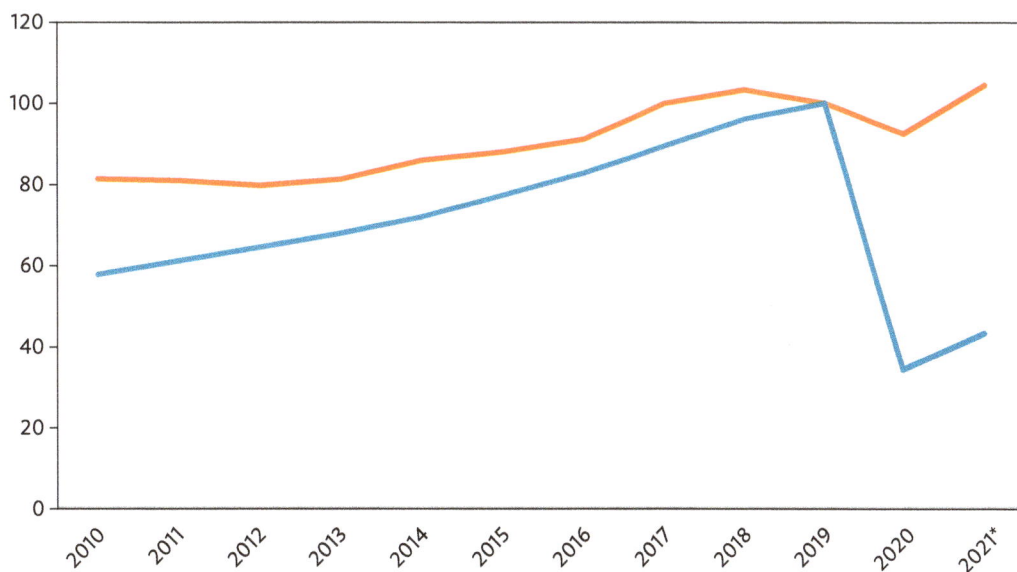

*Forecast estimate.
Source: IATA Economics Airline Industry Financial Forecast Update - April 2021.

Kazakhstan, the Kyrgyz Republic, and the Russian Federation imposed trade restrictions and a temporary ban on the export of socially significant products to the region, resulting in price surges of wheat and other staples (Giap 2020). The precarious state of recovery threatens to erase agricultural productivity gains obtained from harmonization of trade policies and production diversification in the subregion.

## 2.2 | Causes and Responses before and after COVID-19

As supply chain disruptions increased during the COVID-19 pandemic, it also changed the major sources of disruptions from IT outages to human illness (Figure 3). In 2019, just before the pandemic, an international survey of 352 businesses in 65 countries and 15 sectors found that 52% of firms experienced supply chain disruptions during the year. Unplanned IT outages was the top source of supply chain disruption, at 44% of respondents, followed by adverse weather (35%) and cyberattacks (26%). These were then followed by loss of talent/key skills (21%) and transport network disruptions (16%) (BCI 2019).

As the pandemic hit, 73% of respondents encountered some or significant detrimental effect on the supply side, while about 65% did so on the demand side, the survey conducted in 2020 noted (BCI 2020). Moreover, while 5% of firms experienced over 10 disruptions in 2019, this increased to 28% in 2020. The pandemic subsequently changed the major sources of disruptions to factors contributing to seamless

**Figure 3:** **Major Sources of Disruption on Supply Chains before and after COVID-19**
(% of respondents)

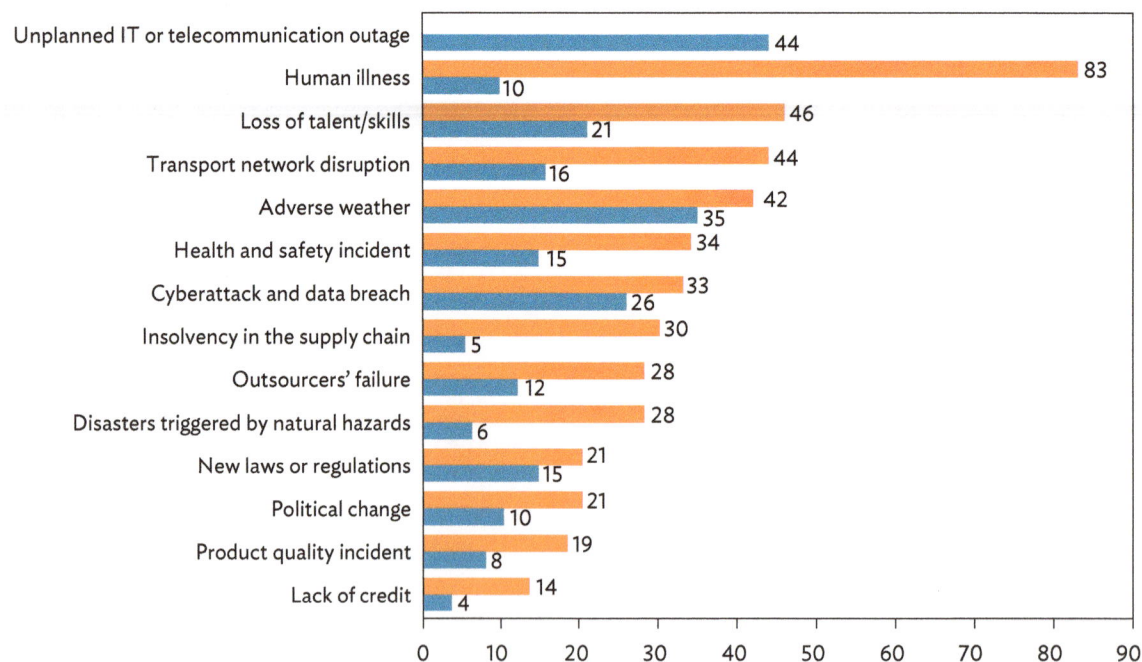

IT = information technology.
Source: BCI (2019) and (2021).

supply chains. The survey in 2021 notes that human illness inevitably became the topmost source of disruption, at 83% of firms, followed by loss of talent/skills (46%), and transport network disruptions (44%) (BCI 2021). The latter two factors were mostly due to secondary impacts of the pandemic, as lockdowns and quarantines caused movement restrictions.

Moreover, traditional disruptions also remained as concerns, as 42% and 33% of firms noted adverse weather and cyberattacks or data breaches as major sources of disruptions, respectively, higher than in the previous year. Cyberattacks are also blamed for the secondary impacts of the pandemic, as fraudsters used COVID-19-related topics in phishing attacks. In the first quarter of 2020, for instance, phishing attacks increased 600%. The pandemic also worsened financing conditions as the share of firms that chose the lack of credit as a source of disruption rose to 14% in 2020 from 4% in 2019.

Conversely, the pandemic prompted many businesses to adopt digital technologies for mapping supply chains and conducting due diligence. Before the pandemic, the consequences of disruptions were mainly loss of productivity (50% of respondents), followed by customer complaints (42%), increased costs (40%), and loss of revenue (36%), resulting from IT outages, adverse weather, and cyberattacks. While loss of revenue ranked fourth previously, it moved to first during COVID-19, followed closely by loss of productivity, both at about 76%. Delayed cash flows (67%) and service outcome impaired (64%) were also major consequences of supply chain disruptions. These however resulted mainly from the pandemic.

Businesses responded to supply chain disruptions by diversifying suppliers and increasing technology use. Business continuity arrangements with suppliers have increased during the pandemic.[13] Nearly 80% of organizations now have such arrangements to manage supply chain disruption, up from 71% in 2019 (Figure 4) (BCI 2021).

**Figure 4: Business Continuity Arrangements and Use of Technology** (% of respondents)

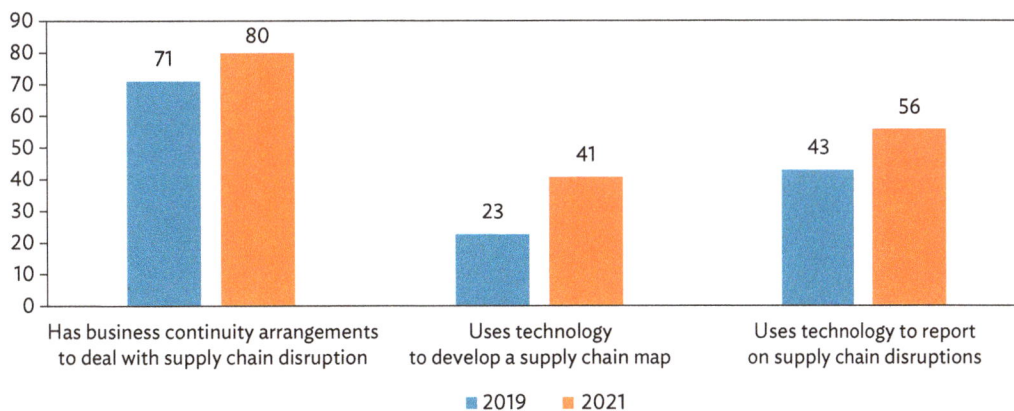

Source: BCI (2019) and (2021).

---

[13] Business continuity refers to plans to deal with difficult situations such as disasters triggered by natural hazards, cyberattacks, losing key employees, etc., so business can continue to operate with minimal disruptions (thebci.org).

Global supply chains have been tested during the pandemic more than many organizations have experienced in their lifetime. Organizations have had to remodel supply chains, reviewing their manufacturing models, returning to stockpiling, reducing reliance on lean inventories, and at times changing all suppliers in the supply chain during the pandemic to ensure business continuity. About 57% of respondents in 2020 planned to diversify their supplier base post-COVID-19. Two-thirds of organizations planned to source goods more locally post-pandemic, with a fifth reporting they will move a considerable number of suppliers more locally (BCI 2020). While another fifth planned to engage in more stockpiling post-pandemic, many are using local sourcing as a more cost-effective way of procuring supplies quickly and efficiently.

Reliance on technology to manage supply chains has also increased, mostly in supply chain mapping. As many key suppliers were unable to meet contract requirements and other businesses discovered backup sources, the importance of visibility of the supply chain or mapping supplier networks increased. While technology uptake has been increasing even before the pandemic, for the first time, more than half of organizations are now using technology to help streamline the recording and analytics process: about 56% of respondents in 2020 relied on technology to analyze and report on supply chain disruptions, compared with 43% in 2019 (BCI 2021). The use of big data analytics, Internet of Things, and artificial intelligence are becoming the norm in many organizations. More organizations are also centralizing reporting processes to ensure better responses to disruptions. In addition, more than half of organizations (58%) note that COVID-19 has been the reason for investing in new technology and tools.

# 3 Supply Chain Resilience

## 3.1 | Concept

The concept of resilience has been used in various fields of study. In engineering, resilience refers to the tendency of a material to return to its original shape after the removal of a stress that has produced elastic strain; in ecology, it resembles the idea of adaptability, or defined as the ability for an ecosystem to rebound from a disturbance while maintaining diversity, integrity, and ecological processes. It is also used in organizational leadership to refer to qualities beyond education and training that can bring business success to an organization. In economics, resilience has often referred to how economies bounce back from economic or financial crisis, focusing on the policies that enable countries to recover. This is similar to supply chain resilience, or how disruptions from trade wars, protectionism, rising costs, disasters triggered by natural hazards, and epidemics, can be minimized with the proper policies and strategies.

The conceptual framework of supply chain resilience proposed by Pettit, Fiksel, and Croxton (2010) suggests that forces of change create supply chain vulnerabilities defined by "fundamental factors that make an enterprise susceptible to disruptions" (Figure 5). This is countered by management controls that create supply chain capabilities, which are "attributes that enable an enterprise to anticipate and overcome disruptions." Capabilities include flexibility in sourcing, adaptability, dispersion of assets, collaboration, and other factors, while vulnerabilities include turbulence such as from disasters triggered by natural hazards, resource limits, supplier disruptions, or connectivity or the degree of reliance on outside entities (Table 2).

Overall, supply chain performance improves when capabilities and vulnerabilities are more balanced. In principle, supply chain resilience increases as capabilities increase and vulnerabilities decrease, but vulnerabilities should be appropriately addressed by supply chain capabilities. Excessive vulnerabilities relative to capabilities lead to excessive risk, while the reverse can impinge on profitability. Pettit, Fiksel, and Croxton (2010) note that as a global supply chain has high levels of connectivity, it should also have strong capabilities in the areas of collaboration, visibility, and flexibility to effectively oversee multiple tiers of suppliers and customers and contribute to more balanced resilience.

Governments can help enhance resilience by providing adequate public goods, for instance, building infrastructure, implementing reforms for ease of doing business, and collaborating with other countries to facilitate cross-border trade. Capabilities thus incorporate public policies and private sector decisions as well as public–private coordination. This would also include regional cooperation among governments for cross-border infrastructure and harmonized customs systems. On the other hand, vulnerabilities may arise from government actions such as restrictive trade policies or export bans.

**Figure 5:** Conceptual Framework of Supply Chain Resilience

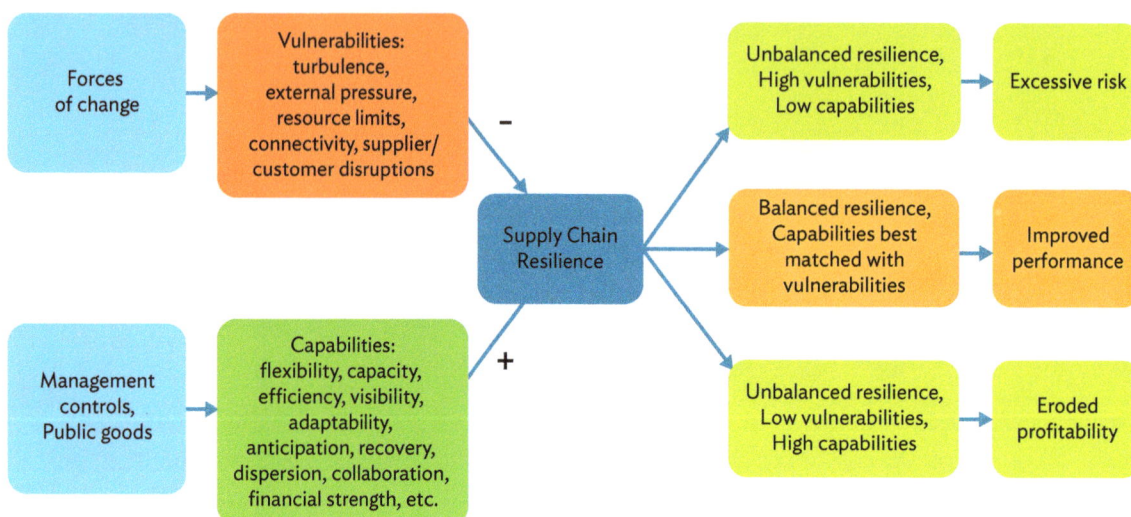

Source: Authors based on Pettit, Fiksel, and Croxton (2010).

**Table 2:** Major Vulnerabilities and Capabilities in Supply Chain Management

| | Type | Examples |
|---|---|---|
| **Vulnerabilities** | Turbulence | Pandemic, disasters triggered by natural hazards, geopolitical disruptions |
| | External pressure | Political/regulatory change, environmental change, price pressures |
| | Resource limits | Supplier, production and distribution capacity; raw material and utilities availability, human resources |
| | Connectivity | Degree of outsourcing, import and export channels, reliance upon specialty sources |
| | Supplier/customer disruptions | Supplier reliability, customer disruptions |
| **Capabilities** | Flexibility in sourcing/order fulfillment | Multiple sources/uses, alternative distribution channels, inventory management |
| | Capacity | Reserve capacity, redundancy, backup energy sources and communications |
| | Efficiency | Labor productivity, failure prevention, asset utilization |
| | Visibility | Information technology, products, assets and people visibility, business intelligence gathering |
| | Adaptability | Fast rerouting of requirements, lead-time reduction, seizing advantage from disruptions |
| | Anticipation | Forecasting, contingency planning, risk management |
| | Recovery | Crisis management, resource mobilization, communications strategy |
| | Dispersion | Distributed capacity and assets, decentralization of key resources, diversified markets |
| | Collaboration | Communications, postponement of orders, risk sharing with partners |
| | Financial strength | Financial reserves and liquidity, insurance, portfolio diversification |

Source: Pettit, Fiksel, and Croxton (2010).

## 3.2 | Emerging Vulnerabilities

The COVID-19 pandemic has revealed considerable weaknesses and market failures in the production and distribution of critical goods such as medical supplies and foods in particular. The pandemic (*turbulence* in Table 2) laid bare the risks of globalization and global supply chains. Concentrated trade networks (*connectivity*) and the strategy of limiting inventories (*resource limits*) contributed to vulnerabilities in supply chains. High global value chain participation also left Asia and the Pacific vulnerable to restrictive trade measures (*external pressure*).

At the start of the pandemic, the immediate need for PPE at a global scale revealed severe resource limits in supply and production. Countries scrambled to find alternative producers, realigning firms in various industries to produce needed quantities. Poor connectivity and concentrated trade networks mainly around the PRC further added to the vulnerabilities. As governments enforced lockdowns and mobility restrictions, PPE supply disruptions within countries rippled around the world. This also included other medical supplies and intermediate products, particularly pharmaceutical and food ingredients.

Finance shortages (lack of "*financial strength*") worsened resource constraints. As global demand dropped quickly and unexpectedly, traders failed to fulfill payments to banks, which thus became more reluctant to lend. Lack of trade finance hinders the flow of commercial imports and exports of essential goods such as food, drugs, and medical equipment, disproportionately hitting small and medium-sized firms producing primary goods. When supply chain disruptions are coupled with a credit crunch, trade credit such as inter-firm open account transactions becomes an influential channel for domestic and cross-border shocks to propagate with profound impact across industries around the globe (Raddatz 2010; Lee et al. 2021).

**Figure 6: Products Affected by COVID-19-Related Trade Measures**

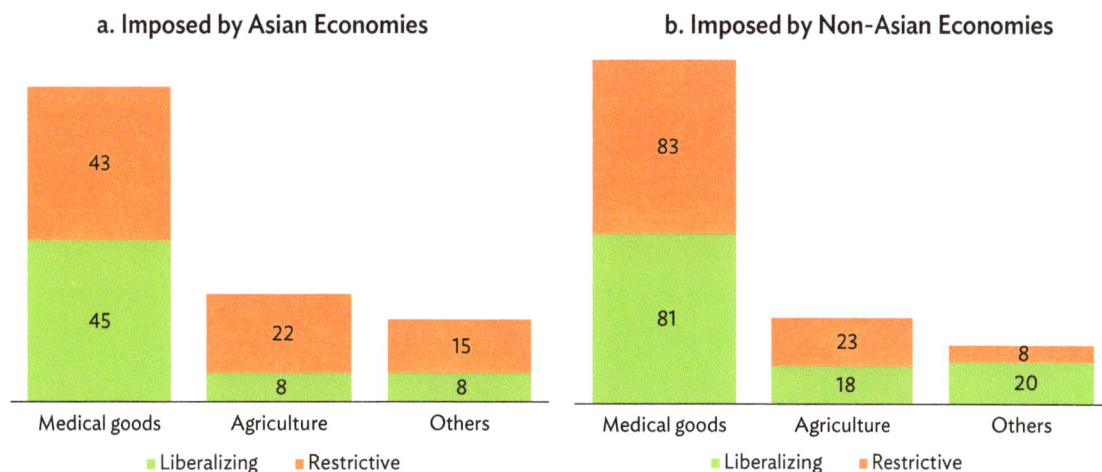

Source: Asian Development Bank calculations using data from International Trade Centre. https://www.intracen.org (accessed April 2021).

Trade policy crucially anchors the smooth functioning of international production networks. During the pandemic, however, many economies imposed trade-restricting policies on medical and agriculture goods (Figure 6). Asian and non-Asian economies imposed restrictive trade measures on PPE and other medical goods. The prevalence of lockdowns, work stoppages, and mobility restrictions, including maritime transport, disrupted agricultural supply chains and prompted some countries to limit agricultural exports to protect domestic demand.

## 3.3 | Existing Capabilities

To ensure unimpeded production and movement of essential goods in this unprecedented crisis, authorities built and strengthened capabilities across various areas. Building on past lessons, existing national and regional mechanisms and initiatives helped raise capabilities in *"collaboration," "efficiency," "capacity,"* and *"recovery"* of supply chains and economies; demand was urgent for new measures, while the existing ones required adjustment.

Following the SARS epidemic, ASEAN countries, along with the PRC, the Republic of Korea, and Japan, prioritized cooperation initiatives around international travel, public education, and alert and response capabilities to prevent and manage infectious disease (ASEAN Plus Three 2003). ASEAN also partnered with these three countries to establish the ASEAN plus Three Emergency Rice Reserve in 2011 to assure food security and mitigate price spikes during crisis.[14] In 2020, 1,000 tons of rice were donated from the Republic of Korea reserves to the Philippines in response to a typhoon, in addition to 600 tons for Myanmar, while Japan donated 300 tons from its reserves to Cambodia in response to flood, drought, and the COVID-19 pandemic (apterr.org). Within ASEAN, member countries also devised a sectoral mutual recognition arrangement for good manufacturing practices for pharmaceutical and other products to avoid duplicate inspections and facilitate trade and accessibility to medicinal products (asean.org).

Trade facilitation measures, meanwhile, have involved global, regional, and national institutions. The World Trade Organization (WTO) Trade Facilitation Agreement entered into force in early 2017 after being ratified by two-thirds of WTO members. The agreement has provisions for expediting movement, release, and clearance of goods, with measures for effective cooperation between customs and other agencies on trade facilitation and customs compliance. It also provides for technical assistance and capacity building in trade facilitation.

Various trade facilitation programs had been under way at subregional institutions in the Asia and Pacific region along with national modernization efforts in this area, including adoption of national single windows. However, inadequate digitalization in many cross-border agencies, ports, and terminal operators still hinder the flow of goods.

---

[14]    ASEAN Plus Three Emergency Rice Reserve. apterr.org.

In Central Asia, the Central Asia Regional Economic Cooperation (CAREC) Integrated Trade Agenda 2030 is an overarching strategy in the subregion for infrastructure connectivity and policy harmonization in trade and transport facilitation, tourism, and economic corridors. In September 2020, the Regional Trade Group and Customs Cooperation Committee underscored the importance of keeping trade open and maintaining the momentum of regional cooperation under that agenda. CAREC countries are also developing initiatives for expanding services trade and e-commerce to hasten recovery from the pandemic (ADB 2021a).

In South Asia, trade facilitation is also one of the priorities of the South Asia Subregional Economic Cooperation (SASEC) program. SASEC assistance has helped simplify trade processes, promote border agency automation, develop "through transport" agreements, build trade-related infrastructure, and build capacity (ADB 2021a). During the pandemic, countries in the region simplified customs procedures, waiving the need for paper documents and scaling down customs involvement. Some also waived tariffs and fees on essential goods and terminal charges (Pangilinan and Reddy 2020).

The Greater Mekong Subregion (GMS) Program is another subregional platform that coordinates trade facilitation and transport connectivity. In 2018, an "Early Harvest" of the GMS Cross-Border Transport Facilitation Agreement was launched, where transport permits were issued and accepted along certain routes and border crossings in Cambodia, the PRC, the Lao People's Democratic Republic (PDR), Thailand, and Viet Nam (ADB 2019). To ease barriers to transport and trade that have increased in the COVID-19 pandemic, GMS countries continued to coordinate and exchange information on the status of border crossing points and implemented new measures as needed (ADB 2021a).

# 4 Case Studies on Critical Goods—Supply Chain Issues Emerged during the Pandemic

## 4.1 | Vaccines and Personal Protective Equipment[15]

More than a year and a half into the COVID-19 pandemic, economic reopening and recovery crucially depend on vaccination programs substantially lowering the risk of new outbreaks. However, many factors, including limited vaccine supply, logistics challenges, lack of funding and staff resources for vaccination, and vaccine hesitancy hamper efforts to immunize a meaningful share of populations quickly to effectively curb the pandemic. Since early in the pandemic, countries around the world encountered critical shortages of PPE and other essential medical devices, particularly ventilators to support patients with severe respiratory conditions. Panic buying, hoarding, and misuse made the early situation worse, aggravated by export bans on medical supplies and PPE to curb local shortages. Thus, securing sufficient supplies of vaccines and PPE remains an important challenge in many parts of the world in the success of the rollout and in sustaining essential health services.

### 4.1.1 COVID-19 Vaccines

COVID-19 vaccines have been developed at an unprecedented speed. As of July 2021, 20 vaccines had been authorized for use by at least one country, with more than 130 candidates currently in clinical trials.[16] In Asia, the PRC and India have developed their own vaccines, while a few other countries have their own candidates in clinical trials.

As of July 2021, around 200 countries had started rolling out vaccines. While North America has been able to dispense 100 doses per 100 people, vaccination in other regions, particularly those in the low-middle income remains sluggish. Asia and the Pacific was able to improve vaccination with 44 doses administered per 100 people, anchored by strong efforts in the PRC and Singapore (Figure 7). Vaccine availability, however, remains a significant threat to recovery paths around the world. The planned production for authorized vaccines covers only about 40% of the world population under a two-dose regime in 2021—or 5.4 billion doses. For 2022 and 2023, the situation might improve, as 23 billion doses are anticipated to become available annually (Figure 8).

Various trade measures imposed by major vaccine-producing countries, giving priority to domestic demand, have hampered global deployment of vaccines. Increased demand for vaccines due to the recurrence of the pandemic in India delayed COVAX's deliveries of the AstraZeneca-Oxford vaccines produced by the Serum

---

[15] This section draws from the latest updates from Park et al. (2020); and Park et al. (2021).
[16] COVID-19 Vaccine Tracker. https://covid19.trackvaccines.org (accessed 5 July 2021).

**Figure 7:  COVID-19 Vaccine Doses Administered per 100 People**

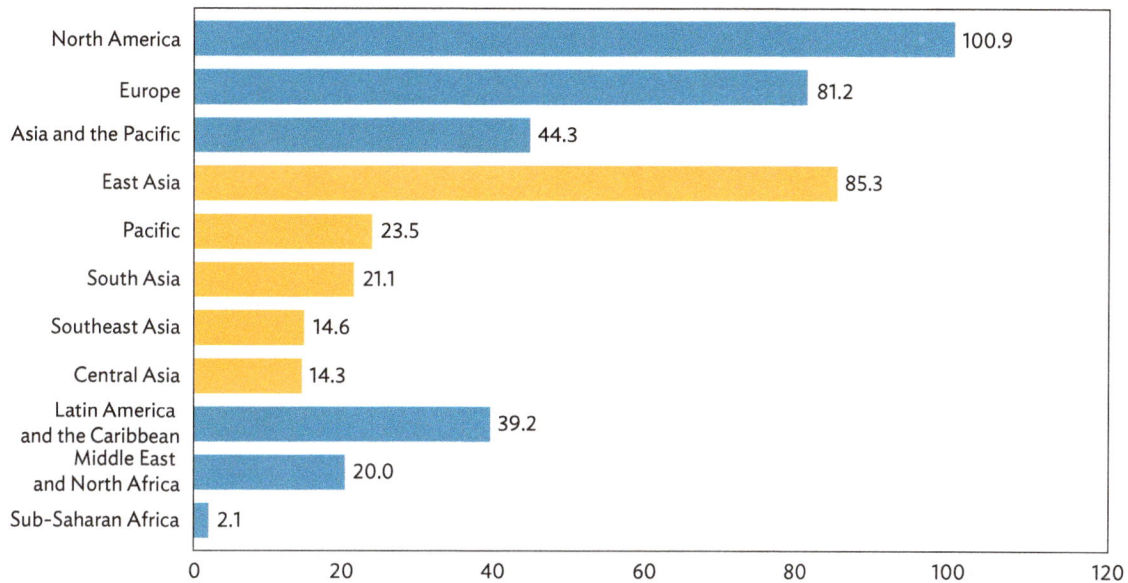

|  |  |
| --- | --- |
| North America | 100.9 |
| Europe | 81.2 |
| Asia and the Pacific | 44.3 |
| East Asia | 85.3 |
| Pacific | 23.5 |
| South Asia | 21.1 |
| Southeast Asia | 14.6 |
| Central Asia | 14.3 |
| Latin America and the Caribbean | 39.2 |
| Middle East and North Africa | 20.0 |
| Sub-Saharan Africa | 2.1 |

Source: Bloomberg. Covid-19 Tracker. https://www.bloomberg.com/graphics/covid-vaccine-tracker-global-distribution/ (accessed 5 July 2021).

**Figure 8:  COVID-19 Vaccine Production Capacity**
   (billion doses, authorized vaccines only)

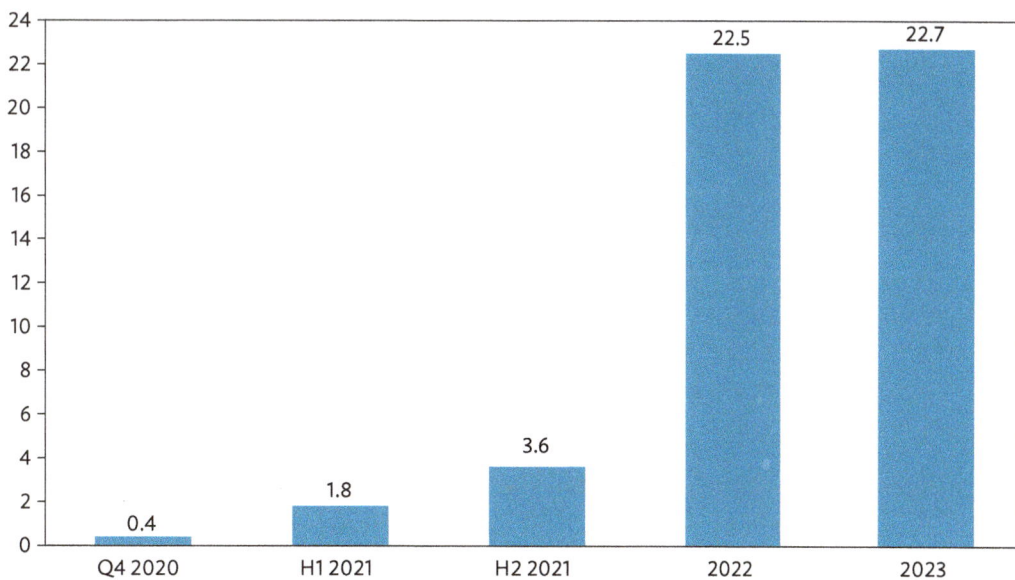

| Period | Billion doses |
| --- | --- |
| Q4 2020 | 0.4 |
| H1 2021 | 1.8 |
| H2 2021 | 3.6 |
| 2022 | 22.5 |
| 2023 | 22.7 |

H = half, Q = quarter.
Source: United Nations Children's Fund. COVID-19 Vaccine Market Dashboard (accessed 5 July 2021).

Institute of India in March and April 2021 (Gavi 2021). The mobilization of the Defense Production Act in the United States enabled the government to reserve vaccine production lines and stockpile essential raw materials (Whitehouse.gov 2021). This may have reduced exports of vaccines and raw materials to other countries. The European Commission enforced an export authorization mechanism for manufacturers with whom the European Union (EU) made advanced purchase agreements. This required manufacturers to provide information on production for the EU and for exports outside the EU, to be used to assess whether exports threaten execution of the advanced purchase agreements (European Commission 2021).

A large COVID-19 vaccination campaign is challenging for many developing countries in Asia and the Pacific. Apart from sufficient funding for vaccine procurement, a successful campaign requires transport, storage, and logistics infrastructure; capacity in health facilities; sufficient medical personnel; safety monitoring; and strong public awareness and advocacy campaigns. Many countries' existing immunization programs may not be ready for the new vaccines and require new guidance, including the adaptation of the current programs to allow large vaccination programs for adults and elderly people. A well-managed logistics system is particularly important to efficient vaccine rollout. The World Health Organization estimates that more than 50% of vaccines generally may be wasted globally every year because of temperature control, logistics, and shipment-related issues (WHO 2005).

Complicating the COVID-19 vaccination is that some vaccines must be kept and transported in extremely cold temperatures. Overall, the cold chain ensures that the quality and safety of products are maintained from origin, throughout distribution, and to the patient (Figure 9). Each level of the vaccine cold chain system requires different equipment, from storage to transport. Along with proper refrigeration, components of the vaccine itself include glass containers, syringes, vials, and other secondary packaging. In general, freezer rooms, freezers, refrigerators, and cold boxes are needed to deploy vaccines. These are ideally found at nationally, provincially, or at the district level. Meanwhile, at the peripheral level (health facilities), refrigeration, cooling components, and cold boxes are utilized. In addition, vaccine carriers may be utilized, depending on the needs of the vaccine.

Developing economies need to address several logistics issues to successfully immunize their populations.

- **Low air transport capacity.** Closed airports and lack of flights during the pandemic have created additional bottlenecks. The International Air Transport Association says 8,000 cargo jumbo jets would be needed to deliver a single dose to the world's 7.8 billion people, compared with the roughly 400 still flying (Mancini 2020). Current air transport capacity is thus far below the minimum required to address the transport demands of COVID-19 vaccines. Further, the global route network has shrunk dramatically from 24,000 city pairs pre-pandemic (IATA 2021).[17]

- **Security and border management.** This includes arrangements to ensure shipments remain secure from tampering and theft at all points in the supply chain. Distribution of a new vaccine creates

---

[17]    As of March 2021, the risk of low air transport capacity had been mitigated somewhat by slow vaccine production, which eases the strain on air cargo capacity, and a significant amount of the vaccines are manufactured and consumed locally: for example, within the PRC, the EU, India, the Russian Federation, and the United States, requiring overland transport or short-haul flights (Kurian 2021).

**Figure 9:  The Flow and Main Components of the Vaccine Cold Chain**

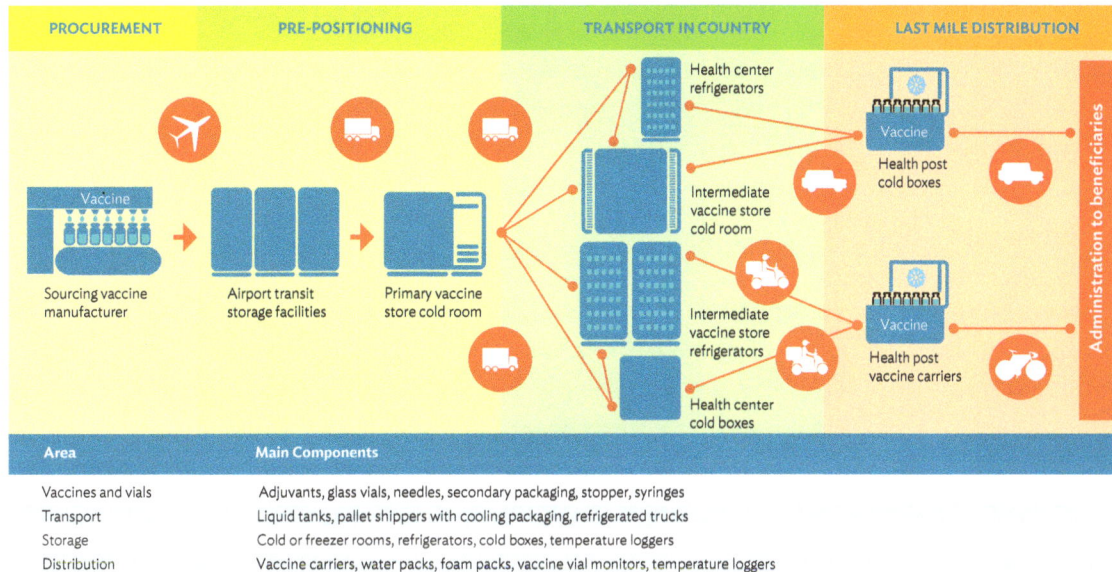

| Area | Main Components |
| --- | --- |
| Vaccines and vials | Adjuvants, glass vials, needles, secondary packaging, stopper, syringes |
| Transport | Liquid tanks, pallet shippers with cooling packaging, refrigerated trucks |
| Storage | Cold or freezer rooms, refrigerators, cold boxes, temperature loggers |
| Distribution | Vaccine carriers, water packs, foam packs, vaccine vial monitors, temperature loggers |

Sources: Reproduced by the Asian Development Bank based on Medium (2020) and cited in ADB (2021b; World Health Organization (2015).

additional requirements at the border for customs and public health authorities to eradicate illicit trade of counterfeit medical goods. Well-coordinated and timely regulatory approvals, inspection, and clearance by customs and health authorities are essential. Priorities for border processes should include introducing fast-track procedures for overflight and landing permits for operations carrying the COVID-19 vaccine and considering tariff relief to facilitate the movement of the vaccine.

- **Inadequate temperature-controlled supply chains.** Temperature-controlled supply chains are limited in developing economies, making it hard to accommodate the various temperature requirements of the different vaccines. UNICEF estimates that the poorest countries would need additional funding of $133 million to support in-country vaccine logistics and cold chain equipment (UNICEF 2020). Except for a handful of advanced economies, many countries in Asia and the Pacific are not ready for vaccine distribution, with temperature requirements as low as –80°C, although the region's preparedness significantly improves for conventional cold chain.

- **Improper handling of vaccines and lack of information.** Losses are substantial from mishandling of vaccines during storage and in transit through various stages in the cold chain. In most countries with immunization programs, breakdowns in refrigeration during transport and storage of vaccines in remote rural areas or at regional and national central stores have led to great losses of vaccine. The losses are often caused by poor temperature management; low levels of technology; and insufficient skills, knowledge, and management capacity. Earlier studies already make clear that qualified and vigilant personnel are critical for successful cold chain management, together with efficient and reliable equipment (Guinebault 1986).

- **Vaccination in rural areas and the last mile.** The toughest challenge in vaccine distribution is delivery to a country's farthest-flung areas. An estimated 25% of vaccines are lost as last-mile challenges strain existing health and cold chain infrastructure (SciDev.Net 2020). For example, only 10% of health-care facilities in the world's poorest countries have a reliable electricity supply (WEF 2018). Health workers also face poor infrastructure and a lack of proper transportation, which reduces the frequency of outreach visits to these areas. Establishing well-functioning cold chains is a heavy burden for developing Asia, where more than half of the population resides in remote and rural areas.

## 4.1.2  Personal Protective Equipment

At the onset of the pandemic, constraints on production and logistics in the PPE supply chain left it unable to meet a surge in demand (Figure 10). Prices of PPE products rose dramatically: a sixfold increase for surgical masks, threefold for respirators, and a doubling in the price of gowns. Surging demand for masks led to a shortage in nonwoven polypropylene, a key component used to produce the fabric that filters out germs and droplets. An unanticipated increase in orders created a production backlog of key materials and fabric assembly. Reportedly, it would take at least 5 to 6 months to assemble a single machine production line to make the melt-blown fabric needed for the masks. Even if factories could be geared up to meet demand, they were not able to get the equipment to the people who needed it, due to restrictions on the movement of people and goods.

**Figure 10:  Personal Protective Equipment Supply Chain Bottlenecks**

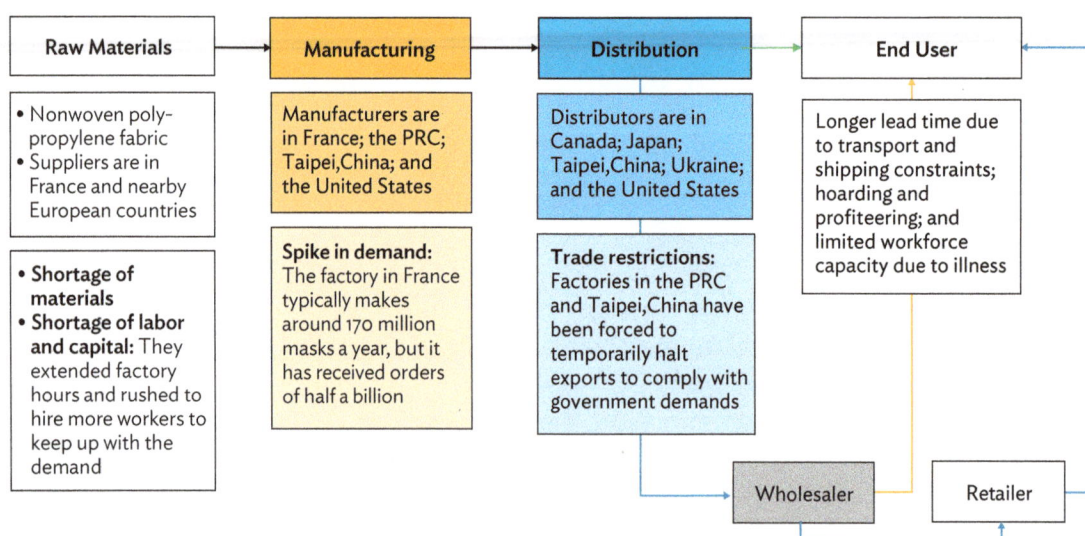

PRC = People's Republic of China.

Note: This figure illustrates the case of face masks produced by Medicom, Inc., a PPE manufacturer based in Canada with offices in the United States; the Netherlands (European arm); and Hong Kong, China (Asian arm).

Sources: Asian Development Bank based on Alderman (2020), Feng and Cheng (2020), Henneberry (n.d.).

However, the surge in PPE demand ultimately spurred a dramatic increase, at least 300%, in global PPE production, mainly driven by mask manufacturing growth of as much as 1,200%. Existing manufacturers were able to expand production capacities, accounting for 50%–60% of the supply increase, while the rest came from a shift in production by similar manufacturers, such as those in textiles and expanded production by smaller local manufacturers (McKinsey & Company 2020).

The pandemic has put a spotlight on the vulnerabilities of global supply chains for critical medical supplies. Important factors that have contributed to the heightened sensitivity of the supply chain to disruptions include the following:

- **Geographic concentration of manufacturers:** The geographic concentration of major manufacturers for vaccines and PPE makes the supply vulnerable to any localized shocks and changes in national security laws and trade policies. For example, during the pandemic, the high dependence on a few major manufacturing centers has led to supply disruptions when major manufacturing facilities in these regional hubs have faced shutdowns, causing disruptions along the entire supply chain for the PPE.

   The PRC accounted for half the global supply of masks, with a daily production of about 20 million units before the outbreak. Germany and the United States (US) remain significant producers of face masks for their corresponding regions. But as the world's largest producer of face masks, the PRC plays a central role in producing and exporting masks to both Asia and the world (Figure 11). Similar patterns in regional clustering are observed for protective gowns and goggles. The PRC, Malaysia, and Thailand are the top-three exporters of gloves. Manufacturers of other types of personal protective equipment that rely on raw materials or products from the PRC have also been affected.

- **Trade restrictions:** The global shortages in vaccines and PPE were worsened by export bans on medical supplies and key materials in a number of countries. As of June 2021, 98 countries globally still have temporary export restrictions in place for PPE and medical products.[18] Such measures mainly applied to banning exports or requiring licenses or permits to export.

- **Other bottlenecks:** Transport and shipping constraints caused by roadblocks and quarantine measures, as well as lower availability of transportation and freight containers, hoarding, profiteering, and limited workforce capacity due to illness, also contribute to the shortage.

---

[18]    ITC Market Access Map. https://www.macmap.org/covid19 (accessed 30 March 2021).

**Figure 11:** Global Trade Networks of Select Personal Protective Equipment Products, 2019

a. HS 630790 Including Surgical Masks:
Textiles; made up articles (including dress patterns), not elsewhere classified (n.e.c.)

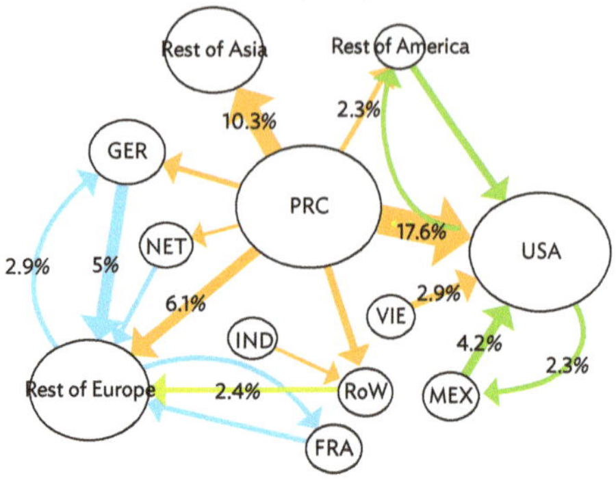

b. HS 392690 Including Respirators:
Plastics; other articles n.e.c

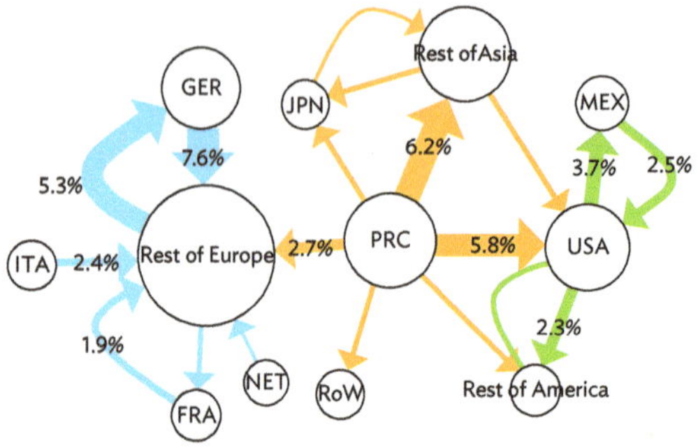

c. HS 621010 Including Surgical Gowns:
Garments; of felt or nonwoven (not knitted or crocheted)

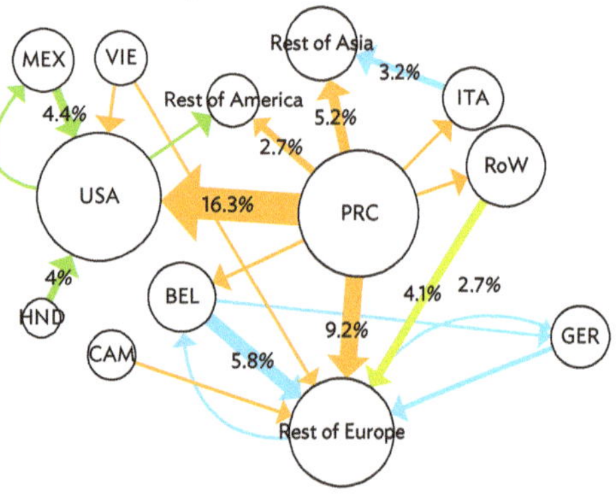

d. HS 392620 Including Protective Suits:
Plastics; articles of apparel and clothing accessories (including gloves, mittens, and mitts)

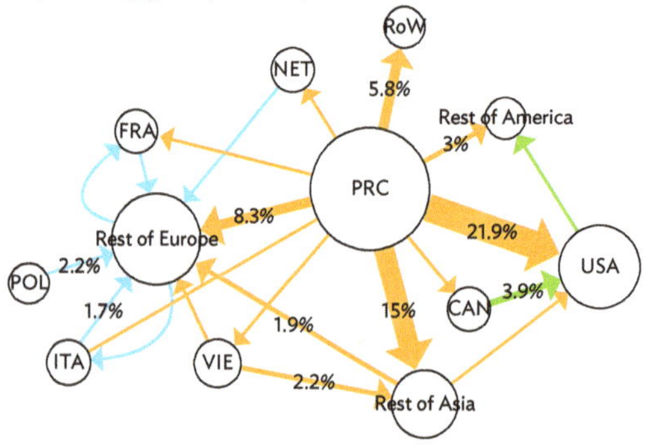

e. HS 900490 Including Protective Goggles:
Spectacles, goggles, and the like; (other than sunglasses) corrective, protective, or other

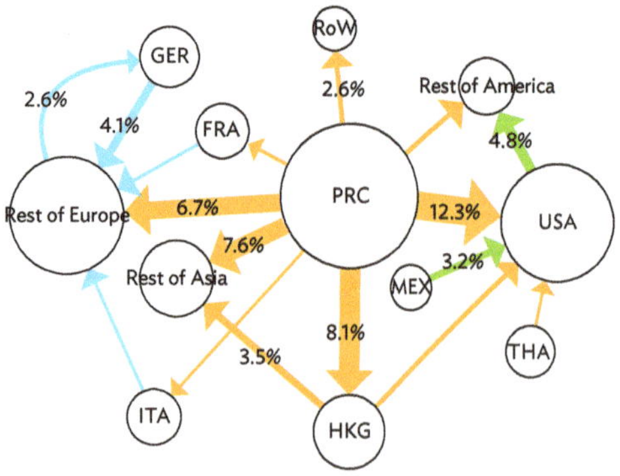

f. HS 401511 Including Surgical Gloves:
Rubber; vulcanized (other than hard rubber), surgical gloves

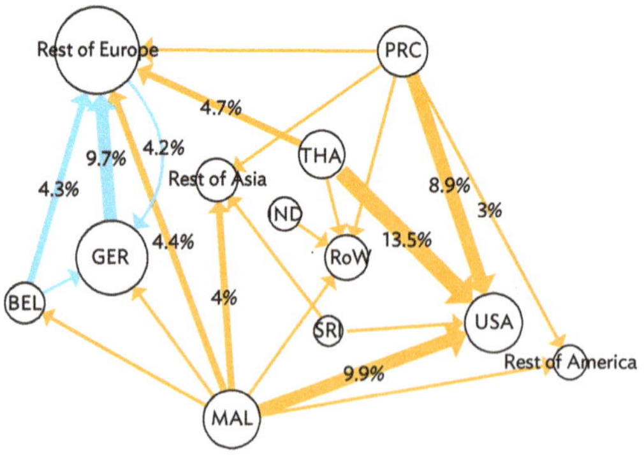

Exports from Americas        Exports from Asia        Exports from Europe        Exports from the rest of the world

BEL = Belgium; CAM = Cambodia; CAN = Canada; FRA = France; GER = Germany; HKG = Hong Kong, China; HND = Honduras; HS = Harmonized System; IND = India; ITA = Italy; JPN = Japan; MAL = Malaysia; MEX = Mexico; n.e.c. = not elsewhere classified; NET = Netherlands; POL = Poland; PPE = personal protective equipment; PRC = People's Republic of China; RoW = rest of the world; SRI = Sri Lanka; THA = Thailand; USA = United States; VIE = Viet Nam.

Notes: The size of the nodes represents the economy's total trade (exports plus imports) of the concerned commodity group. The thickness of the lines represents the value of the flow of goods between economies. Some lines show the share of exports to the total global exports of the commodity group. For clarity, only exports with high values are represented by the lines.

Source: Asian Development Bank calculations using data from the United Nations. Commodity Trade Database. https://comtrade.un.org (accessed 16 March 2021).

## 4.2 | Food Supply Chain[19]

During COVID-19, food supply chains have come under pressure from domestic and international disruptions. Domestically, disruptions in upstream food supply chains arose from mobility restrictions and worker illnesses during planting and harvesting, in addition to hindered operations in processing, trucking, logistics, and trading. Internationally, border closures and export restrictions impede supply of agriculture produce, disrupting cross-border food supply chains, endangering food security and nutrition for countries that rely on imports.

Disruptions in domestic supply chains were significant during the first half of 2020. The implementation of restrictions on domestic transport was most stringent in the region in the first half of 2020, peaking in April (Figure 12). The restrictions also saw a huge drop in the mobility of people. Though domestic transport has been loosening since then, mobility has remained lower compared with the 2019 baseline.

**Figure 12:** **Domestic Movement Restrictions and Mobility in Asia and the Pacific**

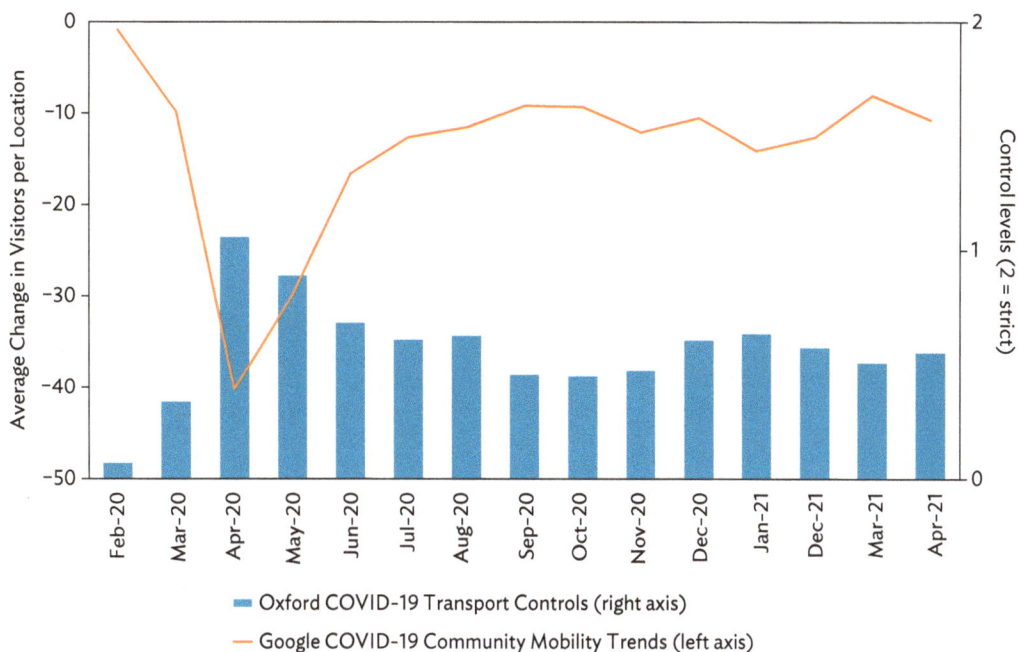

- Oxford COVID-19 Transport Controls (right axis)
- Google COVID-19 Community Mobility Trends (left axis)

Note: Oxford measure is interpreted as 0 = no measures, 1 = some restrictions, 2 = citizens not allowed to use transport. Google mobility trends are interpreted as change in visitors as compared to baseline levels before the pandemic (parks, grocery and pharmacy stores, retail and recreation, workplaces, transit stations).

Source: Asian Development Bank calculations using data from Oxford COVID-19 Government Response Tracker, https://www.bsg.ox.ac.uk/research/research-projects/covid-19-government-response-tracker; and Google COVID-19 Community Mobility Trends https://www.google.com/covid19/mobility/ (both accessed May 2021).

---

[19]    This section draws from the latest updates from Kim, Kim, and Park (2020).

The lockdowns caused immediate, unwanted, and large-scale impacts on entire stages of food supply chains (Figure 13). At the domestic level, travel restrictions prevented local and migrant workers from moving to farms, processing, and packaging facilities, many of which were closed due to quarantine requirements and sick workers. Access to farm inputs—such as seeds, fertilizers, and crop protection products—became challenging. Impacts were larger on labor-intensive food industries, including fruits, vegetables, dairy products, and meat processing. Restrictions in urban transportation and logistics services impaired the movement of goods. High-value perishable farm products, particularly fruits and vegetables, suffered from the limited last-mile delivery from ports or local farms to urban distribution centers and subsequently to point of consumption.

Domestic supply chains also suffered as many of the farm activities are driven by season and value chain activities needed to be undertaken in a timely manner. Any delay in one stage can lead to a larger impact resulting in loss in yield and output (FAO 2020). It was reported that in many places farmers were forced to destroy their produce due to travel restrictions and limited workforce. Restaurant, hotel, and school closures left many farmers with no buyers, again forcing them to destroy fresh vegetables. For example, US dairy farmers had to dump thousands of gallons of milk as the supply chain disruptions prevented them from reaching the marketplace on time. In India, tea planters suffered due to logistical challenges during the height of pandemic (BBC 2020).

Cross-border transport restrictions and export bans disrupted the global supply chain. Maritime transport was particularly hampered by disruption in port facilities, which in turn hindered the distribution of imported foods. Due to the pandemic, additional time and costs were required in cargo handling. For example, health screening was compulsory for crew, and disembarkation was prohibited. Ports were also congested due to lack of workers and transport to clear cargo, leaving refrigerated storage unavailable for fresh foods,

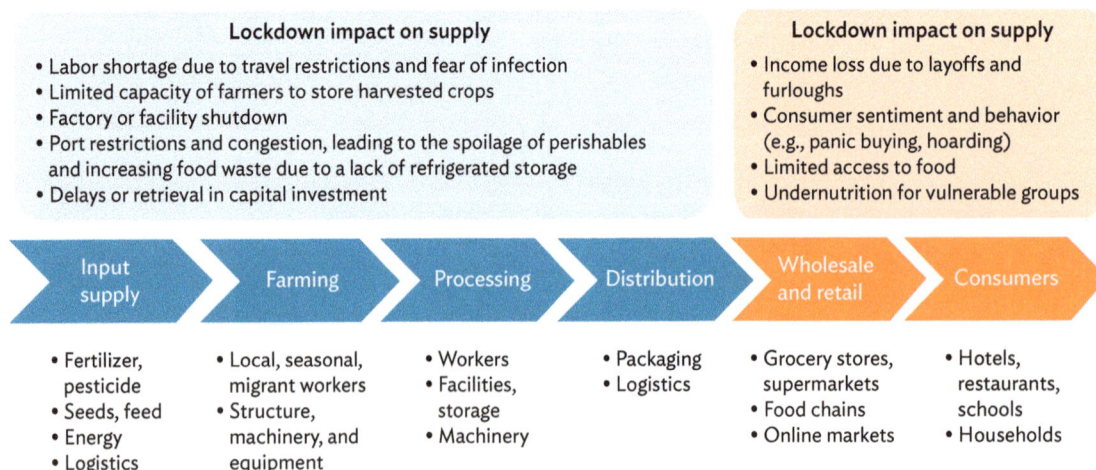

**Figure 13:** **Possible Lockdown Impact on Food Supply Chain**

Source: Authors.

while land transportation to or from ports was not sufficient (North 2020). Extended delays for food containers caused perishables to spoil and increased food waste (see Box 3 for specific cases in select Asian developing countries).

Export bans on basic food items further strained regional supply chains. Since January 2020, 23 countries have imposed some form of export-related measure on agricultural products.[20] Many of these trade restrictions have aimed to ensure stable domestic food supply amid the COVID-19 pandemic. For example,

## Box 3:  Food Supply Chain Disruptions in Select Asian Countries

In **India**, food prices climbed sharply across the country as transportation services froze and fresh supplies became unavailable during lockdown. This hurt the bumper harvest of wheat in northern India, while the western city of Pune, where grapes are produced in abundance, had to seek student volunteers for harvest. In Maharashtra, Asia's largest onion trading market, transporting onion harvests was impeded as the fear of the virus made drivers and workers flee to their homes. Despite high demand for processed food, such as instant noodles, biscuits and snacks, food processing activities halted. Major producers such as Nestle and PepsiCo could not raise production as laborers moved back to their villages (Pothan, Taguchi, Santini 2020).

In **Central Asian countries**, where 70%–80% of intraregional trade is conducted by road, limited road transport disrupted fruit and vegetable distribution. Some border crossings were closed or operated under restricted hours, while drivers were forced to stay home, resulting in a shortage of drivers. Export bans have also affected food supplies in food-importing countries. In **Uzbekistan**, imports of flour and grain fell significantly as Kazakhstan imposed export bans on wheat. Imports of rice, soybeans, and sunflower seeds have also been affected as the Eurasian Economic Union set export bans on various commodities (Eurasianet 2020).

In **Indonesia**, where domestic production has failed to keep up with a rising population, the pandemic has had restricted ability to import amid disruptions in global supply chains and distribution networks. Local disruptions in production and distribution have also occurred, amid oversupply in warehousing, processing, and distribution centers, causing farm-gate prices to decline. Provinces across the country also experienced deficits in key staples such as rice, garlic, sugar, chili peppers, eggs, and corn (Tantau 2020).

During lockdown in the **People's Republic of China**, transport of agricultural inputs was limited and labor was in shortage, while nearly every phase of the distribution channel for agricultural products was disrupted, from local buying to wholesaling, and from cross-region logistics to city consumption. Closures of restaurants and public canteens reduced demand for agricultural products, which led to large amounts of unsold seasonal vegetables and fruits or even unpicked in farms (Fei and Ni 2020).

In **Papua New Guinea**, the pandemic compounded the stress in food systems already apparent from African swine fever and fall armyworm. This may significantly undermine food supply and human nutrition for rural villagers (80% of the population). COVID-19 is expected to disrupt supply chains of imported foods (rice and flour-based foods), as well as food produced domestically (sugar, eggs, poultry, pork-based products, and canned tuna) (Bourke and Kanua 2020).

Source: Bourke and Kanua (2020); Eurasianet (2020); Fei and Ni (2020); Pothan, Taguchi, and Santini (2020); and Tantau (2020).

---

[20]    The International Food Policy Research Institute, in its food export restrictions tracker, accessed July 2021.

Viet Nam, the third-largest rice exporter, and Cambodia, imposed export bans on rice in March and April 2020 while Myanmar suspended the issuance of new export licenses. The Russian Federation, the world's top wheat exporter, banned exports of processed grains from March to June 2020, while Ukraine banned buckwheat exports from April to July. Kazakhstan implemented export restrictions on wheat and other commodities (Laborde and Parent 2020).

Consumption in many Asian developing countries is highly dependent on imports, while only a few exporters account for the majority of external supplies, such as India, Kazakhstan, Pakistan, the Russian Federation, and Thailand. Countries in East Asia and the Pacific are all net cereal importers and nearly all countries in Central Asia depend heavily on imports (Table 3). Given the high concentration in sources of food imports, trade restrictions and logistics disruptions in origin countries undermined food security in many parts of Asia. For example, the wheat export ban by the Russian Federation, the world's largest exporter of wheat, affected Azerbaijan, Armenia, Georgia, and Mongolia, which depend on majority of their wheat imports from the Russian Federation export, while restriction on rice by Viet Nam badly affected rice-importing ASEAN countries. The importing countries in Central Asia were already facing higher import food prices, in part because of depreciating local currencies against the US dollar as global demand for commodities fell. Similarly, Bangladesh, Nepal, and Sri Lanka were vulnerable to trade disruptions originating from India given their high dependence on rice imports from there.

**Table 3:** **Bilateral Trade Flows of Rice and Wheat for Select Importers** (% total imports, 2019)

(a) Rice

| Exporter/Importer | LAO | BAN | NEP | INO | SRI | PHI | MAL | KAZ |
|---|---|---|---|---|---|---|---|---|
| Thailand | 31 | 0 | 0 | 14 | 1 | 6 | 18 | 0 |
| Viet Nam | 67 | 10 | 0 | 7 | 2 | 82 | 57 | 0 |
| India | 0 | 75 | 99 | 0 | 26 | 1 | 9 | 0 |
| Pakistan | 0 | 4 | 0 | 31 | 71 | 3 | 6 | 87 |
| Rest of the world | 2 | 11 | 1 | 48 | 0 | 8 | 10 | 13 |
| Total | 100 | 100 | 100 | 100 | 100 | 100 | 100 | 100 |

(b) Wheat

| Exporter/Importer | AZE | UZB | FIJ | TAJ | AFG | ARM | GEO | MON | KGZ | MAL | PHI |
|---|---|---|---|---|---|---|---|---|---|---|---|
| Russian Federation | 84 | 0 | 0 | 0 | 0 | 96 | 84 | 100 | 3 | 4 | 4 |
| Kazakhstan | 16 | 100 | 0 | 96 | 74 | 0 | 10 | 0 | 85 | 0 | 0 |
| Australia | 0 | 0 | | 0 | 0 | 0 | 0 | 0 | 0 | 33 | 27 |
| United States | 0 | 0 | 0 | 0 | 0 | 0 | 0 | 0 | 0 | 30 | 43 |
| Ukraine | 0 | 0 | 0 | 0 | 0 | 0 | 1 | 0 | 0 | 15 | 15 |
| Rest of the world | 0 | 0 | 0 | 4 | 26 | 4 | 5 | 0 | 12 | 18 | 12 |
| Total | 100 | 100 | 100 | 100 | 100 | 100 | 100 | 100 | 100 | 100 | 100 |

AFG = Afghanistan, ARM = Armenia, AZE = Azerbaijan, BAN = Bangladesh, FIJ = Fiji, GEO = Georgia, INO = Indonesia, KAZ = Kazakhstan, KGZ = Kyrgyz Republic, LAO = Lao People's Democratic Republic, MAL = Malaysia, MON = Mongolia, NEP = Nepal, PHI = Philippines, SRI = Sri Lanka, TAJ = Tajikistan, UZB = Uzbekistan.

Note: Calculation is based on trade volumes in metric tons.

Source: United Nations Commodity Trade Statistics Database. https://comtrade.un.org (accessed July 2021).

As disruptions to domestic and international food supply chains undermined food availability and accessibility, food security risks in Asia and the Pacific were heightened. Losses of employment and income led to a reduction in food consumption, leaving vulnerable groups at risk of hunger and malnutrition. Basic food handouts were often limited and fell short of the nutritional needs of children and pregnant women.

The prices of staple foods such as rice and wheat rose significantly in several developing economies in the region. This was in part due to adverse weather conditions in major producer countries in Southeast Asia, but more broadly driven by disruptions to production and distribution due to the pandemic, combined with panic buying. For instance, prices of rice increased in the initial months of 2020 with international prices increasing around 16% against the previous year's average but eventually staying within the range until 2021 (Figure 14b). In 2021, however, retail rice prices in Bangladesh increased more than 30% year-to-date in April (Figure 14a). Wheat prices have climbed higher, particularly in Central Asia and South Asia. Export bans also impacted international prices of rice and wheat. According to FAO (2021) and U.S. Wheat Associates (2021), the latest increase in the international wheat price since the second half of 2020 is due to several factors such as expectations from the increase in prices of maize and uncertainty in production prospects, rising international freight rates, and drought across vital US farmlands. This is, however, still lower compared with the 2007–2008 crisis which peaked in 2008 with 449 for wheat and 400 for rice (Box 4).

**Figure 14:  Rice and Wheat Prices**

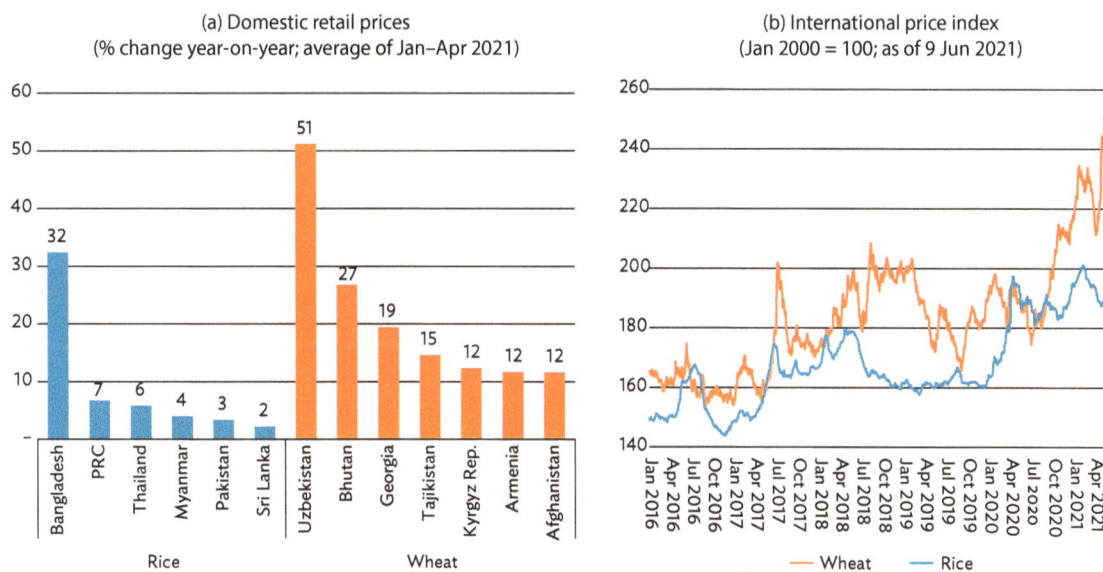

(a) Domestic retail prices
(% change year-on-year; average of Jan–Apr 2021)

(b) International price index
(Jan 2000 = 100; as of 9 Jun 2021)

PRC = People's Republic of China.

Note: International prices are based on "free on board" export quotations in major shipment locations.

Source: International Grains Council. Grains and Oilseeds Index; Agricultural Market Information System (AMIS). http://www.amis-outlook.org/amis-about/en/ (accessed June 2021).

**Box 4:  Comparison with the 2007–2008 Food Price Crisis**

During the food crisis of 2007–2008, global prices of rice, wheat, and maize increased substantially. The cereal price nearly doubled in 2008 compared with the precrisis level in 2005. On the production side, the main causes included poor harvests of wheat due to severe droughts, lower grain stocks, and a rise in oil prices that led to higher prices of farm inputs such as fertilizer (Table). Demand side factors included rapid global economic growth, widespread inflation, and crop demand for biofuels (Wiggins, Keats, and Compton 2010). The depreciation of the United States (US) dollar attracted more cereal import demand, pushing up prices, as the US dollar-denominated price became more affordable.

Restrictive trade policies, such as export bans, also drove up food prices during 2007–2008. Thirty-three countries had trade restrictions, aiming to insulate domestic food prices from the international price surge. However, such policy measures ended up leading to even higher international prices, aggravating food insecurity in net importer countries and inflicting long-term damage on the international food trading system. Moreover, about a third of food policies taken by Asia's developing countries during 2007–2008 were trade-related measures, such as export restrictions and lower import tariffs; the share of such measures increased to 40% in 2008 from 17% in 2007 as food prices soared. Martin and Anderson (2011) estimate that 45% of the increase in rice prices and 30% of the increase in wheat prices resulted from trade restrictions during the crisis. Compared with the 2007–2008 food price crisis, the latest food security concern is primarily driven by supply disruptions and logistics constraints caused by quarantine and lockdown measures. As of June 2021, since the COVID-19 outbreak, 26 countries had implemented restrictive food trade policy measures.

**Table:** Major Factors Contributing to Higher Food Prices in the 2007–2008 Food Crisis and the COVID-19 Pandemic

|  | Food Price Crisis, 2007–2008 | COVID-19 Pandemic (2021, as of 28 June) |
|---|---|---|
| **Main factors** | • **Supply:** Poor harvests, lower grain stocks, higher oil prices ($86/barrel on average; 2007–2008) <br> • **Demand:** Rapid growth of global economy, inflation, crop (maize) demand for biofuels <br> • **Policies:** Export bans and restrictions, lowering import tariffs, restocking <br> • **Other:** Weak US dollar | • **Supply:** Lockdowns and movement restrictions create logistics problems, low energy prices ($39 on average, Jan–Apr 2020), adverse weather conditions <br> • **Demand:** Panic buying, hoarding for staple foods <br> • **Policies:** Export bans and trade restrictions |
| **Trade restrictions** | • Adopted by 33 countries <br> • Share in world market of calories: 19% <br> • On rice: 17 countries including CAM, PRC, IND, INO, PAK, THA, and VIE <br> • On wheat: 13 countries including RUS, KAZ, PRC, UKR, and ARG <br> • On maize: 6 countries including IND, PRC, and UKR | • Adopted by 26 countries (9 are active) <br> • Share in world market of calories: 5% <br> • On rice: 2 countries (VIE and CAM) <br> • On wheat: 6 countries including RUS, KAZ, and UKR |

**Box 4:  *Continued***

| | Food Price Crisis, 2007–2008 | COVID-19 Pandemic (2021, as of 28 June) |
|---|---|---|
| **Food policies in Asian developing countries** | • Total number of policies: 132 (35 in 2007 → 97 in 2008)<br>• Consumer-oriented: 20% (22% → 19%)<br>• Producer-oriented: 43% (53% → 39%)<br>• Trade-related: 34% (17% → 40%)<br>• Macroeconomic: 4% (18% → 2%) | • Total number of policies: 363<br>• Consumer-oriented: 55%<br>• Producer-oriented: 67%<br>• Trade-related: 13%<br>• Macroeconomic: 8% |

ARG = Argentina; CAM = Cambodia; IND = India; INO = Indonesia; KAZ = Kazakhstan; PAK = Pakistan; PRC = People's Republic of China; RUS = Russian Federation; THA = Thailand; UKR = Ukraine; US = United States; VIE = Viet Nam.

Note: Average oil prices are calculated using West Texas Intermediate spot prices; Consumer-oriented policies mainly include social protection, market management, and nutrition and health assistance; Producer-oriented policies mainly include production support and market management.

Source: Wiggins, Keats, and Compton (2010); Laborde and Parent (2020); Food and Agriculture Policy Decision Analysis database. http://www.fao.org/in-action/fapda/fapda-home/en/ (accessed June 2021); Market Access Map. https://www.macmap.org/ (accessed June 2021).

The pandemic significantly affected household food consumption through household income and mobility to groceries, restaurants, and other retail food shops. As slower economies led to job losses and reduced working hours, household incomes declined. Lockdowns and restrictive stay-at-home measures were also limiting access to diverse sources of adequate and nutritious food, especially in countries and communities hit hard by the pandemic.

The pandemic impact on food demand varied depending on the type of food along the food value chain. Panic buying and hoarding drove up prices of certain staple foods at the onset of lockdowns in some countries. Farmers in short value chains, such as for staple crops, benefited from steady demand, while those in medium-sized value chains, such as perishable crops, faced lower demand due to consumer income losses and closure of food service industries (Learning Lab, ISF Advisors, and the Feed the Future Initiative 2020). Disruptions in agriculture supply chains disproportionately affected vulnerable households, including smallholder farmers and small businesses in the food service industries and informal workers, who were more likely to lose their jobs.

The pandemic-induced economic slowdown had significant impact on vulnerable employment, particularly in the developing economies. Around 80% of the global workforce was affected by full or partial workplace closures. The International Labour Organization (ILO 2021) estimates that the pandemic caused a loss of 8.8% of global working hours (equivalent to 225 million full-time jobs) in 2020, compared with the precrisis level.[21] This loss was four times more than what was experienced during the global economic crisis of 2009.

---

[21]   The figures should not be interpreted as numbers of jobs actually lost, although reduction in work hours may increase the possibility of unemployment and loss of labor income.

Asia and the Pacific suffered a working-hour loss of 7.9% (equivalent to 140 million full-time jobs), most of it in Southern Asia.

Informal sector workers in the region (7 in 10 workers) were at high risk given their limited access to social protection and low wages, requiring many to perform multiple jobs to sustain incomes (Figure 15) (ILO 2020). South Asia shows the highest share (89%) in informal employment, followed by Southeast Asia (76%), and Central Asia (59%). Bangladesh, India, and Nepal, where at least 9 in 10 workers are informal, were at greater risk of impoverishment because of the crisis. In these subregions, the share of women in the informal sector is also very high. Earlier studies pointed to evidence that female income share exert positive influence on household spending on food (Hopkins, Levin, and Haddad 1994; Frazao 1992). Income of informal workers is estimated to have fallen 22% in the region in the first month of the COVID-19 crisis, causing relative poverty rates of informal workers to rise to 36% from 22% before the crisis (ILO 2020).[22]

**Figure 15:  Informal Employment** (% total employment, latest available years)

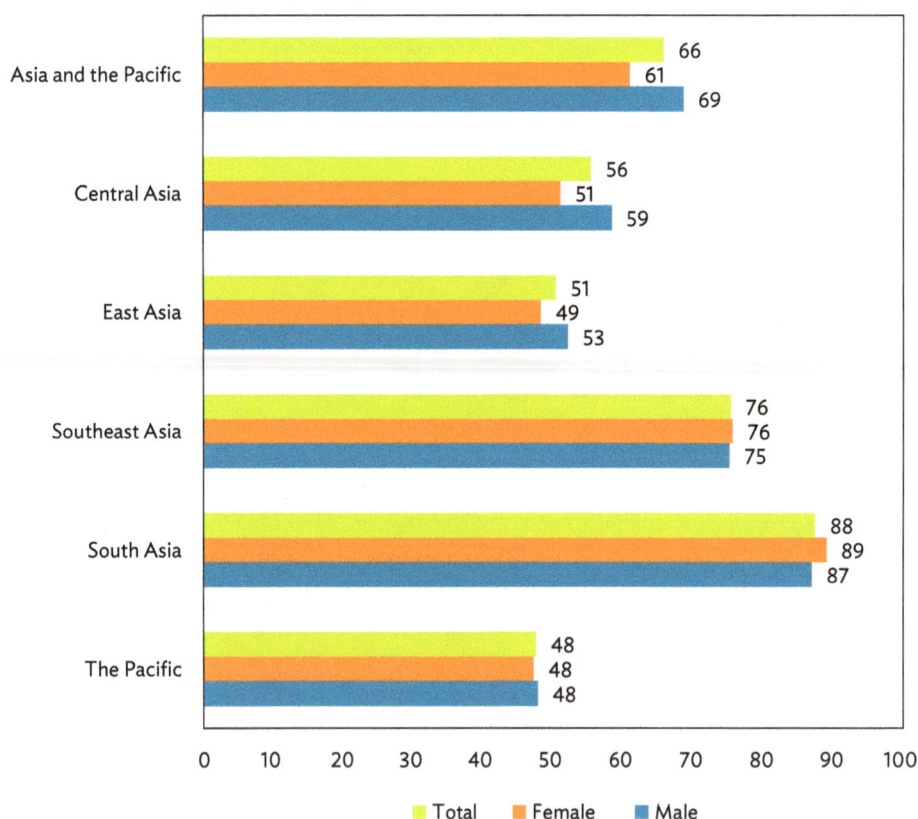

Note: Employment figures include both agriculture and nonagriculture activities.

Source: International Labour Organization. ILOSTAT. https://www.ilo.org/ilostat/ (accessed June 2021).

[22]    Relative poverty is defined as the proportion of workers with monthly labor income that falls below 50% of the median monthly labor income in the population.

At the start of the pandemic, the hardest hit economic sectors were assessed to be accommodation and food services, manufacturing, wholesale and retail trade, and real estate and business activities, according to the ILO's assessment (ILO 2021). Wholesale and retail trade and accommodation and food services, accounting for 18% (170 million workers) of total employment in the region, has been severely impacted by almost full closure, worsened by a fall in demand (Figure 16). More than half of workers in these sectors are also female in all subregions, except for South Asia. Manufacturing (with 14% of total employment in the region) has also suffered severe domestic and global value chain disruptions. This includes automobiles and textiles, clothing, and leather and footwear, among others.

**Figure 16:** **Employment Share by Sector** (% total employment, latest available years)

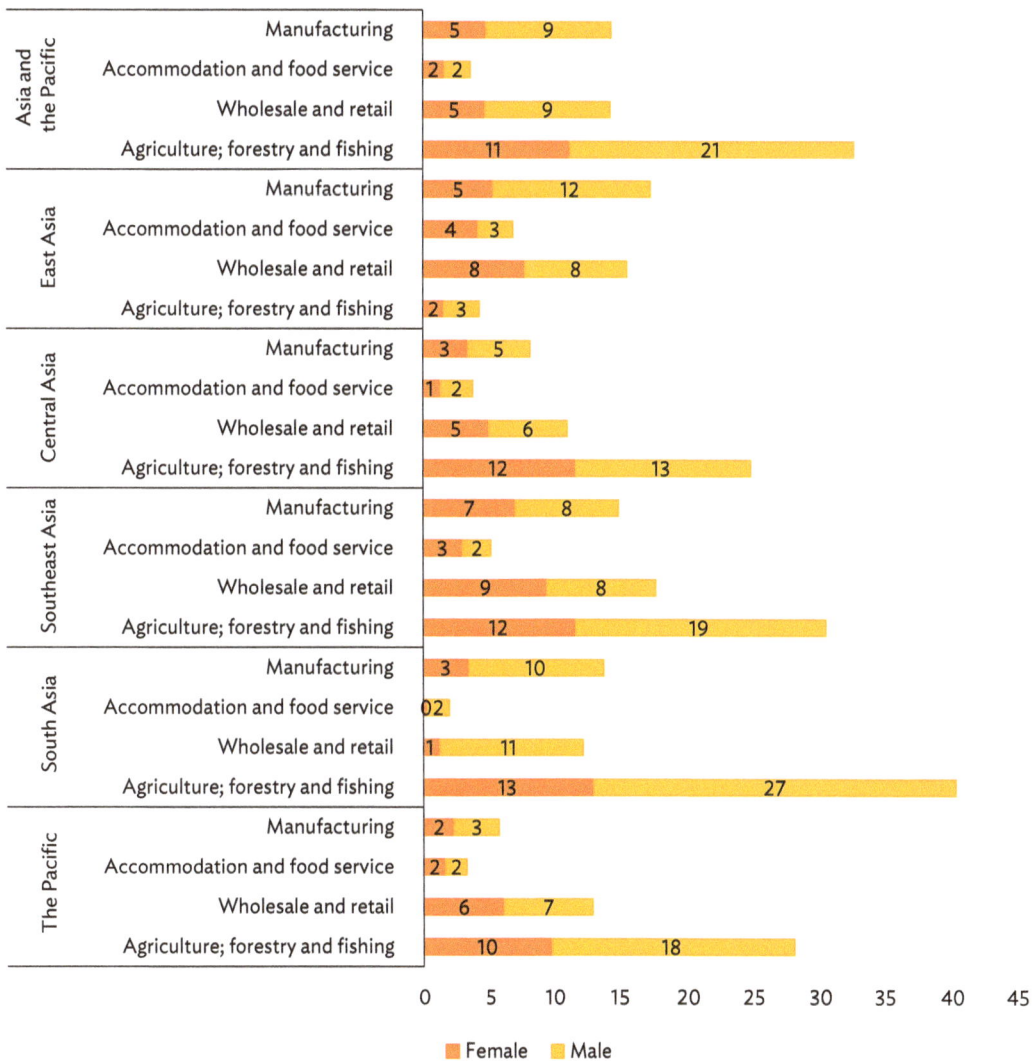

Note: Employment figures include both agriculture and nonagriculture activities.

Source: International Labour Organization. ILOSTAT. https://www.ilo.org/ilostat/ (accessed June 2021).

In agriculture, even though the sector's economic risks are assessed lower, workers were at higher risk of job losses or reduced working hours as agriculture supply chains remain disrupted. This is because agriculture is the largest sector in the region, accounting for 37% (266 million workers) of total employment, and a majority of waged agricultural workers are employed seasonally or casually and without social security or unemployment benefits (Hurst, Termine, and Karl 2005).

Past economic crises have also highlighted that migrant workers face higher unemployment risk. A fall in wages and employment of international migrant workers in host countries may significantly reduce remittances, which can be exacerbated by greater difficulty in transferring funds to home countries due to mobility constraints. Remittance-dependent households in developing countries will likely be hit hard and their capacity to secure affordable food and basic nutrition compromised. As a result, domestic food production can be hurt, because half of remittances are spent on agriculture-related expenses in rural communities (Ponsot et al. 2017). In addition, quarantine measures have disproportionately affected internal (rural-to-urban) migrants in countries such as India, where lockdowns and travel restrictions have created a huge mass of stranded, unemployed internal migrants struggling to return home.[23]

---

[23]    The number of internal migrants is two-and-a-half times that of international migrants. India and the PRC each have over 100 million internal migrants (World Bank 2020a).

# 5 Policy Implications

The COVID-19 pandemic has provided many hard-earned lessons and created a paradigm shift in keeping supply chains more resilient. Lean supply chain management once known for efficiency may be no longer a valid strategy in certain sectors without taking into account potential risks for crises like the COVID-19 pandemic. With every part of the world encountering wide and deep repercussions, regional and global "collaboration" has become even more important among many other capabilities toward supply chain resilience. The case studies also highlight the importance of open trade regimes and trade facilitation, digitally enabled customs initiatives, targeting assistance to vulnerable sectors, and the roles of multilateral institutions.

## 5.1 | Global and Regional Cooperation

The COVID-19 pandemic has exposed the weakest or weaker links in vaccine and PPE supply chains. Given acute shortages in global supply of vaccines and PPE, swift international support and cooperation for building a seamless pipeline to ensure continuity of supply is critical. International cooperation and multilateral approaches to facilitate vaccine procurement and distribution will be particularly important to ensure equitable global access, including lower-income developing countries.

During COVID-19, many regional cooperation measures came into practice to mitigate the adversities. About two-thirds of 20 Asia-Pacific Economic Cooperation (APEC) member economies implemented new trade facilitation measures, such as electronic submissions of trade-related documents and information, to mitigate supply chain disruptions caused by closed workplaces, rising infections, and social distancing. Almost all APEC economies expedited simplifying customs procedures, similar to priority lanes for essential goods, to address congestion at major ports (Bobenrieth 2020). Subsequently, to assure wide availability of vaccine, the COVAX facility to pool the procurement efforts and distribution of vaccines was instituted as a credible global health cooperation. ADB's Asia Pacific Vaccine Access Facility is also designed to support equitable distribution of COVID vaccines among its developing member countries. ADB also mobilized assistance for food and nutrition that targeted vulnerable groups across the region. ADB launched the Rapid Emergency Supplies Provision Project for the Philippines that provided installments of food to vulnerable households. In India, ADB's COVID-19 Active Response and Expenditure Support Program contributed to social protection for more than 800 million people, including farmers, women, senior citizens, and families below the poverty line (Kim, Kim, and Park 2020).

Further efforts to strengthen data sharing, mutual acceptance and recognition of manufacturing practices, drug registration, and inspection and evaluation would improve the efficiency and transparency of regulatory decision-making for vaccination. It is important to improve transparency along global supply chains, identify a list of critical components and their sources, and mobilize alternative sources and options. An efficient, low-burden mechanism for governments and private sector partners to share situational and supply information can help.

## 5.2 | Open Trade and Trade Facilitation

Trade openness will be a key element for economic recovery. The crisis laid bare the vulnerabilities of supply chains as highly integrated economic activities were affected by transport disruptions and other trade restrictive measures. Countries should refrain from using export restrictions and other nontariff measures. They should also increase transparency on trade restrictions brought during and in the aftermath of COVID-19. The impact of protectionist measures on the global economy and international trade have never been positive. Kutlina-Dimitrova and Lakatos (2017) estimate that annual global real income of 0.3% or $211 billion is lost annually after 3 years if all countries decide to withdraw from tariff commitments made under different trade agreements.

Trade facilitation measures helped ease trade flows of essential goods at the onset of the pandemic (Box 5). As the health crisis is prolonged, ramping up trade facilitation initiatives is crucial. Countries should prioritize implementation of the WTO's TFA and the Framework Agreement on Facilitation of Cross-Border Paperless Trade in Asia and the Pacific, to help countries recover post COVID-19. Greater implementation of the WTO-TFA agenda can help reduce trade costs by 5%–16% for Asia and the Pacific, with maximum cost reductions achieved through digital, paperless trade facilitation (ADB and ESCAP 2019). These help to promote supply chain connectivity and accelerate trade flows as documents and information are transferred digitally across participating countries. For instance, the ASEAN Single Window has seen steady progress in implementing live operations. In December 2019, all member states joined in the live operations to obtain

---

**Box 5: Trade Facilitation for Essential Goods during the COVID-19 Pandemic**

During the pandemic, countries implemented measures to ease trade flows. Indonesia, for example, enacted the Acceleration Programme for Handling COVID-19 Goods Importation that includes setting up a task force, integrating systems, relaxing procedures, and establishing fiscal facilities. An online national single window is being utilized to hasten applications and show real-time information on applications, processing, and approvals in the system. Goods under the system such as vaccines and vaccine kits, raw materials, and production equipment, are exempt from import duties and are quickly released from customs, while individuals and the private sector are also free to import subject to obtaining import licenses from health and food ministries.

In Georgia, the government enacted an Interagency Coordination Council in January 2020 to handle activities related to COVID-19. The government also set up a similar one stop shop outfit with reduced transit formalities, paperless environment, and an effective control mechanism based on risk management. The temporary admission of storage equipment is also exempt from all taxes, duties, and fees.

As a vaccine-exporting country, India set up the COVID Vaccine Response Team to act as a single point of contact for all vaccine shipment clearances. The system included a single window help desk for both exporters and importers, 24/7 customs clearance facility, automated systems for release of consignments, and duty exemption at ports and airports.

Sources: Martediansyah (2021), Uridia (2021), Ananth (2021).

preferential tariff treatment based on the ASEAN Trade in Goods Agreement's electronic Certificate of Origin. All member states are expected to be on board in 2021, with the ASEAN Single Window expanding to include other e-documents such as phytosanitary, animal health, and food safety certificates. A subset of ASEAN members—Cambodia, the Lao PDR, Malaysia, Singapore, Thailand, and Viet Nam—have also embarked on the ASEAN Customs Transit System for smooth and cost-efficient movement of goods across countries.

Logistics support and proper handling of vaccines are integral to successful immunization. Many developing countries in Asia and the Pacific are not ready for the enormous logistical challenges to distribute COVID-19 vaccines rapidly and safely under stringent temperature requirements. Since much wastage is also caused by mishandling of vaccines, having well-trained personnel is a must, along with properly designed cold-chain management policies and procedures.

## 5.3 | Digital Technology

Greater global and regional efforts should also be exerted in utilizing digital technologies to enhance monitoring, market search, and developing supply chains. For instance, online platforms can be used for direct marketing of agricultural produce and to reduce food waste and farmers' losses by facilitating market search and reducing multiple layers of intermediaries. Advanced technologies can also help record land use on crop production, market arrival, traded stocks, and weather information to facilitate collaborative planning among agricultural value chain actors.

Monitoring PPE use and distribution as well as centralizing visibility of orders can also benefit from digital technologies. Moreover, while lean manufacturing and just-in-time inventory systems have cut costs in PPE supply chains, this has resulted in an overall reduction in stocks. This system should be replaced with maintaining adequate PPE stocks with sufficient surge capacity to respond to health emergencies. Digital systems can also be employed to monitor vaccine procurement and distribution as well as vaccinated populations globally.

As the pandemic has accelerated the road to digital, paperless trading, more work is needed to leverage information and communication technology (ICT) to streamline customs procedures and electronic exchange of information, implement national and regional single windows for document submissions and clearance, and introduce e-registration of travel documents. Trade finance can also adopt digital platforms to benefit small borrowers and lenders. Technologies used by fintech firms such as Internet of Things and blockchain can significantly reduce the costs of due diligence and information asymmetry in transactions. The digital transformation can also benefit integrated transport management systems and digital logistic platforms.

Adopting ICT for trade facilitation reform has become a necessity for paperless trade, and requires complex coordination of legal and technical standards to realize international interoperability and efficiency. Standards for data, for instance, are driven by the UN Centre for Trade Facilitation and Electronic Business Reference Data Models and the World Customs Organization data model, while legal frameworks for cross-border data exchange are steered by the UN Commission on International Trade Law, which serves as the model law for arbitration of disputes in international transactions.[24] Moreover, modern supply chains are based on relationships between data entities in international sales, transport contracts, and demand a reformulation of measures that adhere to broadening channels such as cross-border e-commerce and trade policy compliance and delivery through digital means (Atkinson 2020). Multilateral institutions and national trade facilitation committees that already exist in many economies can be the platform for coordination. In addition, as regional trade agreements increasingly include WTO provisions on digital trade and e-commerce, it runs the risk of exacerbating the "spaghetti bowl" effect of these agreements. Countries should work toward sufficient homogeneity of regional trade agreements to facilitate their multilateralization (López González, and Ferencz 2018).

## 5.4 | Assistance Targeted to Vulnerable Economies and Groups

International efforts should include targeting assistance to vulnerable economies and sectors. The poorest and most vulnerable people are likely to be more exposed to infection risks, job and income losses, and inadequate medical treatment. Reforms in agriculture can include targeted support to smallholder farmers, including improving their access to digital infrastructure and training, rural financing, marketing opportunities, and value chain infrastructure. Micro, small, and medium-sized enterprises (MSMEs) are particularly vulnerable to the economic and trade impact of COVID-19.

Many PPE and supply manufacturers in the region are also MSMEs. Some have been forced to close and lay off employees, while many have faced cash flow difficulties. Many small businesses are also experiencing supply chain disruptions, sales and trade reductions, and liquidity and working capital constraints. Trade finance programs can aid in facilitating trade of these small producers in the supply chain. Strengthening regional cooperation can also help low-income economies gain access to vaccines.

## 5.5 | Role of Multilateral Institutions

Multilateral institutions played key roles in responding to the pandemic and cushioning its health and economic impacts. ADB's initial response of $6.5 billion was raised to $20.0 billion early in 2020 to support countercyclical measures in its developing member countries. This included for instance $1.5 billion each for India, Indonesia, the Philippines, and Thailand for disease containment and social protection support for economically vulnerable groups. On the production side, ADB expanded its operations to support supply chains in food and medical supplies. Such support is needed to increase production capacity in the whole supply chain network for medical supplies, while countries also need guarantees to make advanced

---

[24] The goal of the UN Centre for Trade Facilitation and Electronic Business reference data models is to be the semantic hub for all electronic data requirements in the international supply chain from end to end. It covers all sectors of activities including materials management, commercial, logistics, transport, agriculture, health, insurance, finance, payments, customs, etc., and can be used by anyone free of charge. The World Customs Organization data model provide data requirements that serve to meet the procedural and legal needs of cross-border regulatory agencies such as customs, controlling export, import, and transit transactions (World Customs Organization (WCO). WCO Data Model. http://www.wcoomd.org/DataModel).

payments. These programs to enhance social protection and provide liquidity support to farmers and other small producers facing financial stress should continue—and can readily be increased as the need arises.

COVID-19 vaccines are manufactured in only a handful of countries, and the majority of countries around the globe would be importing them. Moreover, vaccines need to be stored and transported under controlled conditions, as noted. In response, the World Customs Organization and WHO jointly developed a harmonized list of vaccines and related products such as syringes, swabs, and freezing equipment to guide customs and border agencies on facilitating imports of these products. These institutions also responded earlier in creating a harmonized list for PPE, such as surgical and plastic gloves, masks, goggles, protective garments, and disinfectants.

In response to the trade finance shortage, the WTO and major multilateral banks, including the International Finance Corporation, the European Bank for Reconstruction and Development , ADB, and others, in July 2020 declared a crisis in trade finance and allocated resources to mitigate. ADB also ramped up its Trade and Supply Chain Finance Program to help these supply chains expand capacity. Since April 2020, its trade finance program has supported over 9,000 transactions valued at $8.6 billion, while supply chain finance has supported about 3,400 transactions valued at $277 million, including medical supply and food security and agriculture-related transactions.

Multilateral institutions also play a key role in advancing free trade and helping countries implement trade facilitation measures. An integrated global economy requires open trade regimes, harmonized customs systems with interoperable digital infrastructure, as well as full implementation of the WTO Trade Facilitation Agreement. Weak and fragmented regulatory systems cause delays and increase costs of trading across borders. The multilateral development banks' coordinating role should continue to support regional efforts at trade facilitation policies. ADB's subregional programs provide an institutional venue for these initiatives. Helping economies build regulatory capacity as well as acquire the needed digital infrastructure should also be supported.

# REFERENCES

Alderman, L. 2020. As Coronavirus Spreads, Face Mask Makers Go into Overdrive. *The New York Times.* 6 February. https://www.nytimes.com/2020/02/06/business/coronavirus-face-masks.html.

Anbumozhi, V. 2020. Resilient Supply Chains for Post-COVID Asia. Economic Research Institute for ASEAN and East Asia. https://www.eria.org/news-and-views/resilient-supply-chains-for-post-covid-asia/.

ASEAN Plus Three. 2003. Joint Statement ASEAN + 3 Ministers of Health Special Meeting on SARS. 26 April. Kuala Lumpur. https://asean.org/joint-statement-of-asean-3-ministers-of-health-special-meeting-on-sars/.

Asian Development Bank (ADB). 2019. *Asian Economic Integration Report 2019/2020: Demographic Change, Productivity, and the Role of Technology.* Manila. https://aric.adb.org/aeir2019-2020.

————. 2021a. *Asian Economic Integration Report 2021: Making Digital Platforms Work for Asia and the Pacific.* Manila. https://aric.adb.org/pdf/aeir/AEIR2021_complete.pdf.

————. 2021b. Getting Ready for the COVID-19 Vaccine Rollout. *ADB Briefs.* No. 166. Manila.

Asian Development Bank and Economic and Social Commission for Asia and the Pacific (ADB and ESCAP). 2019. *Asia-Pacific Trade Facilitation Report: Bridging Trade Finance Gaps through Technology.* Manila: ADB. https://www.adb.org/sites/default/files/publication/523896/asia-pacific-trade-facilitation-report-2019.pdf.

Association of Southeast Asian Nations (ASEAN). 2015. FAQ on Mutual Recognition Agreements on Manufacture of Medicinal Products. https://asean.org/wp-content/uploads/2016/06/31.-October-2015-FAQ-on-the-ASEAN-MRA-on-GMP-Inspection-of-Manufacturers-of-Medicinal-Products.pdf.

Atkinson, C. 2020. Advancing the Digitalization of Trade with Partnerships: National Trade Facilitation Committees as a Platform for Policy Modernization. UNCTAD Transport and Trade Facilitation Newsletter No. 86. Article No. 54. https://unctad.org/news/advancing-digitalization-trade-partnerships-national-trade-facilitation-committees-platform.

Barro, R. J., J. F. Ursúa, and J. Weng. 2020. The Coronavirus and the Great Influenza Pandemic: Lessons from the "Spanish Flu" for the Coronavirus's Potential Effects on Mortality and Economic Activity. *National Bureau of Economic Research.* No. w26866. Cambridge, MA.

*BBC*. 2020. Coronavirus: Five Ways the Outbreak is Hitting Global Food Industry. 13 April. https://www.bbc.com/news/world-52267943.

Bénassy-Quéré, A., Y. Decreux, L. Fontagné, and D. Khoudour-Casteras. 2009. Economic Crisis and Global Supply Chains.

Bobenrieth, K. 2020. Why Trade Is a Critical Response to COVID-19. Asia-Pacific Economic Cooperation Blog. 18 June. https://www.apec.org/Press/Blogs/2020/0618_CTI.

Boehm, C.E., A. Flaaen, and N. Pandalai-Nayar. 2019. Input Linkages and the Transmission of Shocks: Firm-level Evidence from the 2011 Tōhoku Earthquake. *Review of Economics and Statistics.* 101 (1): pp. 60–75.

Bourke, M. and M. Kanua. 2020. Potential Response to COVID-19 in PNG: Support for Food Production. *DevPolicyBlog.* https://devpolicy.org/potential-response-to-covid-19-in-png-support-for-food-production-20200421-1/.

Business Continuity Institute (BCI). 2019. *Supply Chain Resilience Report.* https://www.thebci.org/uploads/assets/e5803f73-e3d5-4d78-9efb2f983f25a64d/BCISupplyChainResilienceReportOctober2019SingleLow1.pdf.

———. 2020. *The Future of Supply Chain.* https://www.thebci.org/uploads/assets/7324b815-9364-47d3-9277ab4ce9aa4c0f/a3e39af5-193d-428d-b603d3cf7e600f39/BCI-0007d-The-Future-of-Supply-ChainSingles-Low.pdf.

———. 2021. *Supply Chain Resilience Report.* https://www.thebci.org/uploads/assets/e02a3e5f-82e5-4ff1-b8bc61de9657e9c8/BCI-0007h-Supply-Chain-Resilience-ReportLow-Singles.pdf.

Centers for Disease Control and Prevention (CDC). n.d. 1918 Pandemic (H1N1 virus). https://www.cdc.gov/flu/pandemic-resources/1918-pandemic-h1n1.html#:~:text=It%20is%20estimated%20that%20about,occurring%20in%20the%20United%20States.

———. 2015. 2014–2016 Ebola Outbreak in West Africa. https://www.cdc.gov/vhf/ebola/history/2014-2016-outbreak/index.html.

———. 2017. SARS Basics Fact Sheet. https://www.cdc.gov/sars/about/fs-sars.html.

———. 2019. 1918 Pandemic (H1N1 Virus). https://www.cdc.gov/flu/pandemic-resources/1918-pandemic-h1n1.html#:~:text=It%20is%20estimated%20that%20about,occurring%20in%20the%20United%20States.

Center for Research on Epidemiology of Disasters (CRED). 2011. 2011 disasters in numbers. http://cred.be/sites/default/files/PressConference2011.pdf.

Ernst and Young. 2020. *Managing the Impact of COVID-19 on India's Supply Chains – Now, Next and Beyond.* https://assets.ey.com/content/dam/ey-sites/ey-com/en_in/topics/government-and-public-sector/2020/09/managing-the-impact-of-covid-19-on-india-supply-chains.pdf.

*Eurasianet.* 2020. Uzbekistan Shores Up Food Defenses as Coronavirus Rages. 4 April. https://eurasianet.org/uzbekistan-shores-up-food-defenses-as-coronavirus-rages.

European Commission. 2021. Export Requirements for COVID-19 Vaccines: Frequently Asked Questions, 30 March. https://trade.ec.europa.eu/doclib/docs/2021/february/tradoc_159414.pdf.

Fei, S. and J. Ni. 2020. *Food Systems and COVID-19: A Look into China's Responses.* FAO. http://www.fao.org/in-action/foodfor-cities-programme/news/detail/en/c/1270350/.

Feng, E. and A. Cheng. 2020. COVID-19 Has Caused a Shortage of Face Masks but They're Surprisingly Hard to Make. *National Public Radio.* 16 March. https://www.npr.org/sections/goatsandsoda/2020/03/16/814929294/covid-19-has-caused-a-shortage-of-face-masks-but-theyre-surprisingly-hard-to-mak.

Food and Agriculture Organization of the United Nations (FAO). 2020. Responding to the Impact of the COVID-19 Outbreak on Food Value Chains Through Efficient Logistics. 4 April. http://www.fao.org/3/ca8466en/CA8466EN.pdf.

———. 2021. Food Price Monitoring and Analysis: International Prices. May. http://www.fao.org/documents/card/en/c/cb4720en/.

Frazao, J. 1992. Food Spending by Female-Headed Households. *USDAERS Technical Bulletin.* No. 1806. Washington, DC: USDA.

*GAVI.* 2021. COVAX Updates Participants on Delivery Delays for Vaccines from Serum Institute of India (SII) and AstraZeneca. 25 March. https://www.gavi.org/news/media-room/covax-updates-participants-delivery-delays-vaccines-serum-institute-india-sii-az.

Giap, B. M. 2020. COVID-19 Pandemic Impacts on Food Security in Central and West Asia: Key Issues and Strategic Options. *ADB Central and West Asia Working Paper Series.* No. 9. November. https://www.adb.org/sites/default/files/publication/656091/cwwp-009-covid-19-impacts-food-security.pdf.

Goentzel, J. 2015. Supply Chain Innovation Critical in Ebola Response. *Supply Chain Management Review.* January/February Issue. https://ctl.mit.edu/sites/default/files/SCMR1501_InnovationStrat.pdf.

Guinebault, A. 1986. Storage and Sterilization Techniques: The Specific Role of the Cold Chain. *Children in the Tropics.* 162–163. pp. 53–68.

Haraguchi, M. and U. Lall. 2015. Flood Risks and Impacts: A Case Study of Thailand's Floods in 2011 and Research Questions for Supply Chain Decision Making. *International Journal of Disaster Risk Reduction.* 14. pp. 256–272.

Henneberry, B. n.d. How Surgical Masks Are Made. *Thomas.* https://www.thomasnet.com/articles/other/how-surgical-masks-are-made/immunization/documents/IIP2015_Module2.pdf.

Hopkins, J., C. Levin, and L. Haddad. 1994. Women's Income and Household Expenditure Patterns: Gender or Flow? Evidence from Niger. *American Journal of Agricultural Economics.* 76 (5): pp. 1219–1225.

Hurst, P., P. Termine, and M. Karl. 2005. Agricultural Workers and Their Contribution to Sustainable Agriculture and Rural Development. FAO. http://www.fao.org/tempref/docrep/fao/008/af164e/af164e00.pdf.

International Air Transport Association (IATA). 2021. Guidance for Vaccine and Pharmaceutical Logistics and Distribution: Edition 5. https://www.wto.org/english/tratop_e/trips_e/techsymp_290621/piaget_pres.pdf.

———. 2021. Outlook for the Global Airline Industry (April 2021 update). https://www.iata.org/en/iata-repository/publications/economic-reports/airline-industry-economic-performance---april-2021---report/.

International Grains Council. https://www.igc.int/en/default.aspx.

International Labour Organization (ILO). 2020. ILO Monitor. COVID-19 and the World of Work. Third edition: Updated Estimates and Analysis. 29 April. https://www.ilo.org/wcmsp5/groups/public/---dgreports/--- dcomm/documents/briefingnote/wcms_743146.pdf.

———. 2021. *ILO Monitor: COVID-19 and the World of Work 7th ed.* Geneva. https://www.ilo.org/wcmsp5/groups/public/@dgreports/@dcomm/documents/briefingnote/wcms_767028.pdf.

International Monetary Fund (IMF). 2021. *World Economic Outlook.* April. Washington, DC.

Keat, H. S. 2009. The Global Financial Crisis: Impact on Asia and Policy Challenges Ahead. In *Federal Reserve Bank of San Francisco Proceedings.* October. pp. 267–276.

Kharas, H. 2020. The Impact of COVID-19 on Global Extreme Poverty. *Brookings.* 21 October. https://www.brookings.edu/blog/future-development/2020/10/21/the-impact-of-covid-19-on-global-extreme-poverty/.

Kim, K., S. Kim, and C-Y. Park. 2020. Food Security in Asia and the Pacific amid the COVID-19 Pandemic. ADB Briefs. No. 139. June. https://www.adb.org/sites/default/files/publication/611671/adb-brief-139-food-security-asia-pacific-covid-19.pdf.

Kose, M. A. and F. Ohnsorge. 2019. *A Decade after the Global Recession: Lessons and Challenges for Emerging and Developing Economies.* Washington, DC: World Bank.

Koshimura, S. and N. Shuto. 2015. Response to the 2011 Great East Japan Earthquake and Tsunami Disaster. *Philosophical Transactions of the Royal Society A: Mathematical, Physical and Engineering Sciences.* 373. No. 2053. 20140373.

Kumar, S. 2012. Planning for Avian Flu Disruptions on Global Operations: A DMAIC Case Study. *International Journal of Health Care Quality Assurance.* 25 (3). pp. 197–215.

Kurian, L. C. 2021. Air Freight Uncompromised on Covid-19 Vaccine Delivery. *The Stat Trade Times.* 10 March. https://www.stattimes.com/news/air-freight-uncompromised-on-covid19-vaccine-delivery-air-cargo/.

Kutlina-Dimitrova, Z. and C. Lakatos. 2017. The Global Costs of Protectionism. *Policy Research Working Paper* 8277. Washington, DC: World Bank. https://documents1.worldbank.org/curated/en/962781513281198572/pdf/WPS8277.pdf.

Laborde, D. and M. Parent. 2020. Food Export Restrictions in the Era of Covid-19. https://public.tableau.com/app/profile/laborde6680/viz/ExportRestrictionsTracker/FoodExportRestrictionsTracker.

Learning Lab, ISF Advisors, and the Feed the Future Initiative. 2020. High-Risk Households Dependent on, and Critical for, Food Supply Chains. 7 May. Rural & Agricultural Finance Learning Lab. https://pathways.raflearning.org/covid-19/high-risk-households-dependent-on-and-critical-for-food-supply-chains/.

Leckcivilize, A. 2012. The Impact of Supply Chain Disruptions: Evidence from the Japanese Tsunami. Job Market Paper. London: London School of Economics and Political Science. https://personal.lse.ac.uk/leckcivi/JobMarketPaperA.Leckcivilize.pdf.

Lee, H., S. A. Yang, Y. Zhang, K. Kim. 2021. Credit Chain and Sectoral Co-movement: A Multi-region Investigation. Manuscript.

López González, J. and J. Ferencz. 2018. Digital Trade and Market Openness. *OECD Trade Policy Papers.* No. 217. Paris: OECD Publishing. https://www.oecd-ilibrary.org/docserver/1bd89c9a-en.pdf?expires=1625470734&id=id&accname=guest&checksum=226EE7244A7C6EA729A8A849D6804EA4.

Mancini, D. P. 2020. Logisticians Grapple to Map Out 'Cold Chain' for Vaccine Campaign. *Financial Times.* 8 October. https://www.ft.com/content/c71d254c-14f3-4226-a3e8-df1ee83e5692.

Martediansyah. 2021. Facilitation Import and Export of Vaccines – Indonesia. Powerpoint Presentation from Webinar on Customs Facilitation for Efficient Cross-border Vaccines Movement. RCI Innovation Seminar Series. Asian Development Bank. 7 April.

Martin, W. and K. Anderson. 2011. Export Restrictions and Price Insulation during Commodity Price Boom. *Policy Research Working Paper.* No. 5645. Washington, DC: World Bank.

McKinsey & Company. 2020. Covid-19 – PPE Demand & Supply Perspectives. https://www.ifc.org/wps/wcm/connect/1d32e536-76cc-4023-9430-1333d6b92cc6/210302_FCDO_GlobalPPE_Final+report_v13_gja.pdf?MOD=AJPERES&CVID=nvPXIAZ.

*Medium.* 2020. Detailed Engineering of the COVID-19 Vaccine Cold Supply Chain. 16 June.

Mefford, R. 2009. The Financial Crisis and Global Supply Chains. https://repository.usfca.edu/cgi/viewcontent.cgi?article=1010&context=fe.

North. 2020. COVID-19: Coronavirus Outbreak - Impact on Shipping *Update*. 15 April. https://www.nepia.com/ industry-news/coronavirus-outbreak-impact-on-shipping/.

Noy, I. and S. Shields. 2019. The 2003 Severe Acute Respiratory Syndrome Epidemic: A Retroactive Examination of Economic Costs. *Asian Development Bank Economics Working Paper Series.* No. 591. Manila: ADB.

Pangilinan, A. and S. Reddy 2020. Coping with the Pandemic in South Asia by Making It Easier to Trade. *Asian Development Blog.* 18 November. https://blogs.adb.org/blog/coping-pandemic-south-asia-making-it-easier-trade.

Park, C-Y., K. Kim, M. Helble, S. Roth. 2021. Getting Ready for the COVID-19 Vaccine Rollout. ADB Briefs. No. 166. Manila: ADB.

Park, C-Y., K. Kim, S. Roth, S. Beck, J. W. Kang, M. C. Tayag, M. Griffin. 2020. Global Shortage of Personal Protective Equipment amid COVID-19: Supply Chains, Bottlenecks, and Policy Implications. ADB Briefs. No. 130. April. https://www.adb.org/sites/default/files/publication/579121/ppe-covid-19-supply-chains-bottlenecks-policy.pdf.

Pau, J., J. Baker, N. Houston, M. L. Clifford. 2018. Building Resilience in Businesses and Supply Chains in Asia. Asia Business Council. https://www.asiabusinesscouncil.org/docs/Supply.pdf.

Pettit, T. J., J. Fiksel, and K. L. Croxton. 2010. Ensuring Supply Chain Resilience: Development of a Conceptual Framework. *Journal of Business and Logistics.* 31 (1). pp. 1–21. https://onlinelibrary.wiley.com/doi/full/10.1002/j.2158-1592.2010.tb00125.x.

Ponsot, F., B. Vásquez, D. Terry, and P. De Vasconcelos. 2017. *Sending Money Home: Contributing to the SDGs, One Family at a Time.* Report to the International Fund for Agricultural Development. June. Rome, Italy: United Nations.

Pothan, P. E., M. Taguchi, and G. Santini. 2020. Local Food Systems and COVID-19: A Glimpse on India's Responses. FAO. http://www.fao.org/in-action/food-for-cities-programme/news/detail/en/c/1272232/.

Raddatz, C. E. 2010. Credit Chains and Sectoral Co-movement: Does the Use of Trade Credit Amplify Sectoral Shocks. *The Review of Economics and Statistics.* 92 (4). pp. 985–1003.

Rushton, J., R. Viscarra, E. Guerne Bleich, and A. McLeod. 2005. Impact of Avian Influenza Outbreaks in the Poultry Sectors of Five South East Asian Countries (Cambodia, Indonesia, Lao PDR, Thailand, Viet Nam) Outbreak Costs, Responses and Potential Long Term Control). *World's Poultry Science Journal.* 61 (3). pp. 491–514.

*SciDevNet.* 2020. The Longest Mile in the COVID-19 Vaccine Cold Chain. 18 November. https://www.scidev.net/global/features/the-longest-mile-in-the-covid-19-vaccine-cold-chain/.

Tajitsu, N. 2016. Five Years after Japan Quake, Rewiring of Auto Supply Chain Hits Limits. *Reuters.* 30 March. https://www.reuters.com/article/us-japan-quake-supplychain-idUSKCN0WW09N.

Tantau, M. 2020. Is Indonesia Facing a Looming Food Crisis?. *The Diplomat.* 5 May. https://thediplomat.com/2020/05/is-indonesia-facing-a-looming-food-crisis/.

U.S. Wheat Associates. 2021. Price Reports – June Report. https://www.uswheat.org/market-and-crop-information/price-reports/.

United Nations Centre for Trade Facilitation and Electronic Business (UN/CEFACT) Reference Data Models. 2017. https://tfig.unece.org/contents/uncefact-rdm.htm.

United Nations Conference on Trade and Development (UNCTAD). 2020. *World Investment Report 2020: International Production Beyond the Pandemic*. New York: UN. https://unctad.org/system/files/official-document/wir2020_en.pdf.

United Nations Children's Fund (UNICEF). 2020. UNICEF Outlining Plans to Transport Up to 850 Tonnes of COVID-19 Vaccines per Month on Behalf of COVAX, in 'Mammoth and Historic' Logistics. https://www.unicef.org/press-releases/unicef-outlining-plans-transport-850-tonnes-covid-19-vaccines-month-behalf-covax.

United Nations Development Group (UNDG). 2015. *Socio-Economic Impact of Ebola Virus Disease in West African Countries: A Call for National and Regional Containment, Recovery and Prevention*. UNDG – Western and Central Africa

Uridia, S. 2021. Facilitation Import and Export of Vaccines – Georgia. Powerpoint Presentation from Webinar on Customs Facilitation for Efficient Cross-border Vaccines Movement. RCI Innovation Seminar Series. Asian Development Bank. 7 April.

Wailes, E., R. Clarete, R. Briones, and F. Pochara. 2012. *Food Security in Asia: The 2007–2008 Food Price Crisis*. Manila: ADB.

Whitehouse.gov. 2021. National Strategy for the COVID-19 Response and Pandemic Preparedness. January. https://www.whitehouse.gov/wp-content/uploads/2021/01/National-Strategy-for-the-COVID-19-Response-and-Pandemic-Preparedness.pdf.

Wiggins, S., S. Keats, and J. Compton. 2010. *What Caused the Food Price Spike of 2007/08? Lessons for World Cereals Markets*. London: Overseas Development Institute. https://odi.org/en/publications/what-caused-the-food-price-spike-of-200708-lessons-for-world-cereals-markets/.

World Bank. 2008. *Global Economic Prospects: Commodities at the Crossroads*. Washington, DC.

———. 2014. *The Economic Impact of the 2014 Ebola Epidemic: Short- and Medium-Term Estimates for West Africa*. Washington, DC. doi:10.1596/978-1-4648-0438-0.

———. 2020a. COVID-19: Remittance Flows to Shrink 14% by 2021. https://www.worldbank.org/en/news/press-release/2020/10/29/covid-19-remittance-flows-to-shrink-14-by-2021.

———. 2020b. COVID-19 to Add as Many as 150 Million Extreme Poor by 2021. https://www.worldbank.org/en/news/press-release/2020/10/07/covid-19-to-add-as-many-as-150-million-extreme-poor-by-2021.

World Economic Forum (WEF). 2018. Over Half of Vaccines Are Wasted Globally for these Simple Reasons. 24 July. https://www.weforum.org/agenda/2018/07/the-biggest-hurdle-to-universal-vaccination-might-just-be-a-fridge.

World Health Organization (WHO). 2005. Monitoring Vaccine Wastage at Country Level: Guidelines for Programme Managers. No. WHO/V&B/03.18. Rev. 1.

———. 2015. The Vaccine Cold Chain. https://www.who.int/immunization/documents/IIP2015_Module2.pdf.